DEPUTY

35 Years as a Deputy Sheriff
From Upstate NY to LA

CLIFF YATES

Dedicated to my loving always supportive
Mom and Dad
Without them none of this would have been
possible

Foreword

When Cliff asked me to write the forward to his new book, my first thought was that I was honored, and the second was what do I write?

Thinking about Cliff, "Yes," is the first word that came to mind. Yes, is Cliff's life philosophy when it comes to anything that is positive. I have known Cliff for over three decades. He has been a very close friend for more than half of my life. I have had the pleasure of working with him during different assignments over the years on the Los Angeles County Sheriff's Department.

Cliff is a very talented and positive person. He is extremely diverse in his interests and endeavors. He is always challenging himself, whether it's sailing, bowling, tennis. He gives it his all. Cliff was my roommate during our early years in the Sheriff's department. When he moved out, he left a few things stored in my basement. My new wife was storing items in the basement and came across a unicycle. She seemed puzzled and asked why I had a unicycle. When I told her that it belonged to Cliff, she said without skipping a beat, "that makes sense." She had only known Cliff for a short time, but she could already sense the type of person he is. A very upbeat person with a zest for living and trying new things. Cliff pursues everything with full throttled passion and does not stop until he masters his new challenges and interests. The one constant in his life has been his passion and love for law enforcement. His career in law enforcement started on the east coast in New York as a deputy sheriff, which eventually brought him to the west coast, working for the Los Angeles County Sheriff's Department, the largest sheriffs department in the country. Moving from his home state of New York all the way across the country to Los Angeles is just another example of Cliff saying, "I'm going to do something new!"

***

I have had the pleasure of attending many of his stand -up comedy performances, and I can honestly say that Cliff is one "funny f**ker!" Whether it is doing a stand-up comedy show and cracking up his audience up or writing a book that is enlightening and motivational. He inspires with the purpose of assisting people in achieving their goals; Cliff is all in with positivity and passion!

When Cliff sees something he likes or discovers a new challenge he wants to undertake, he says "Yes" and does it! From practicing juggling while riding a unicycle, acting in film, doing a podcast on working out, walking on hot coals! Cliff is game.

He is true "A" personality that just goes for it. That is a quality that often attracts a person to a career in law enforcement. Cliff's latest book is about those times and other aspects of his life.

Sometimes the stories are sad and tragic; other times, they will make you smile, laugh, and happy that things worked out!

With Cliff, it is not only about what you are going to do but about what you are going to do next. What will Cliff be doing tomorrow? It is anyone's guess!

This is a memoir. All stories are to the best of my recollection. Some names, details, and locations have been changed to protect the innocent, and me from being sued and or beat up. Some real people and names were left in, because they are just great people. The names of many great people were left out, just to protect their privacy. The names of all mean or bad people were left out or changed.

CONTENTS

MY DAD WAS A COP

From as long back as I can remember, I have memories of my dad getting ready to leave the house for his police job. I used to watch the ritual of him shaving, polishing his gear and donning his uniform before kissing Mom and me goodbye and heading out the door, usually at night.

I was about fifteen years old, fast asleep in our Village of Caledonia, New York home when the silence of the early morning hours was broken by the crackle of the police radio in the hallway. Loud voices and screaming sirens filled the house. My dad was Chief of Police in our little town, so we had a police radio in the hall so my dad could hear it from any room in the house. I was a night owl and always had trouble going to sleep at night, so I liked listening to the radio calls as I eventually went to sleep.

One night, Dad came running down the hall already dressed. "Cliffy get dressed; it's a high-speed chase, and you're going with me." Moments later we were in that big Ford LTD police cruiser, and that police package engine was roaring as we screamed out of the driveway onto Park Place. Dad was the Chief, so he always had a marked unit in the driveway. Dad hit the siren, and the rotating red lights lit up the night and flashed across the trees that lined our street. As we approached State Street Route 5, my dad yelled, "There they are!" as three to four Livingston County Sheriff cars and the Village of Avon Police car zoomed past just off the bumper of a grey station wagon. As our right turn screeched on to Route 5, the sight of the five police cars with their rotating police lights in front of us was quite the scene. It was a warm summer night at about 3 am, and the pursuing officers had their windows down because I could hear the rushing wind as they broadcasted their current pursuit location. "It's a stolen car," my dad said as he jumped on the accelerator after negotiating the left turn at the town monument. My dad got on the radio, "300 is in the pursuit." 300 was my dad's call sign indicating the Chief of Police. We must have been going close to 100 mph, and we were not gaining on the chase cars in front of us.

The chase was continuing on Route 5 about to leave the Village of Caledonia when in a flurry of activity, it was over. I couldn't believe how fast we went from being in the chase to seeing the stolen car in the ditch, hearing yelling and breaking glass, and the driver getting dragged out of the driver's window. It was over. After the station wagon went into the ditch, the deputies ran up and broke out the window with their flashlights and dragged the driver out, handcuffing him. There wasn't another car or person on the street—just this police scene of lights, sirens, crackling radio, squealing tires, and the breaking of glass. "Your first high-speed chase of a stolen car," my dad said as we drove from the scene back to our house and back to bed. But not to sleep. Who could sleep after that? Being in a high-speed chase I imagine is like heroin; it's addicting, and you want more.

This was Livingston County, made up of small villages with varying populations from two to five thousand. My dad was Chief of Police for the Village of Caledonia with a population of about three to four thousand. He had two full-time police officers and several part-time officers. The department had two marked police cars, and one was my dad's car that he parked in our driveway every night because he was on call twenty-four seven. On weekend nights, the full-time officers would use both cars. Like most of the village police departments, they would go out of service at about midnight during the week, and around three am on the weekends. After that, the County Sheriff would handle the calls for the village departments.

My police life is going to take on some stark contrast, and I want you to get the perspective difference when I go from policing rural upstate New York, to south-central Los Angeles. But hang on—I'm still in high school. I haven't even decided to be a cop yet.

This is my story, but since this chapter is about my dad being a cop, I would be remiss in not mentioning that my dad was a super cop. Some of the things he did as a street officer and Chief of Police are just amazing. His reputation was far and wide. And he was always loved by the officers that worked with and for him. He always backed his officers 100%.

My dad has some amazing accomplishments as a police officer. Just a few days after joining the Caledonia Police department he had a part-time officer not in uniform riding with him. It was late at night when they stopped a local resident for speeding. The guy pulled over in front of his house. My dad was writing the ticket while the part-time officer was keeping an eye on the lone driver. My dad looked up from writing the ticket to see the driver holding a gun to the head of the part-time officer. My dad got out of the car, and when the driver wouldn't drop the gun, my dad shot him in the arm, causing him to drop it. The guy picked up the gun and said, "Ok Yates, you want it. Now your gonna get it!" as he raised the gun and pointed it at my dad. My dad then shot the guy in the stomach several times. He dropped the gun and staggered backward before collapsing in the front yard of his house. The guy lived.

My dad's first police job was as a deputy with the Livingston County Sheriff's Department. The department which would be my first police job too. Even while working a metropolitan area like Los Angeles, locating a rolling stolen vehicle was a good arrest. My dad, stopped three stolen cars in one night while working for Livingston County. He stopped a group of mafia guys driving through Livingston County with a trunk full of loaded dice (weighted so the same number would come up when rolled).

My dad was a super cop.

HIGH SCHOOL

I was an extremely skinny kid in high school. I was bullied and pushed around because of my weight. Some might think that is why I went into police work, to get revenge because I was bullied, but that was not the case. Because I was so skinny and picked on, I began weight training and bodybuilding. And I was always attracted to entertainment and standup comedy. I memorized comedy acts I saw on tv and would do them for everyone in my class. I would do them for the football team and basketball team. Because of my comedy, I was accepted by all the groups. I had athlete friends, drug kid friends, popular and outcast kid friends.

I really wanted to play sports and be on the teams with my buddies. I tried to play football. I played two years of junior varsity, or should I say I went to the practices and got the shit beat out of me. I was just too small to play football. I had a basketball rim and backboard over our garage. I would practice shooting baskets for hours on end. I would set up lights on a step ladder so I could shoot at night. I would shovel snow from the driveway and shoot all winter. I was an extremely good shot. When I tried out for the team, I guess my lack of ball-handling and defense skills kept me from making the team. I was really devastated and depressed about it.

The coach liked me, and I guess because of my comedy reputation, he asked me if I wanted to announce the home games. I was excited about this. I had a thing for microphones as it was. I had a couple of tape recorders and was always fascinated with talking into a microphone. So every Friday home game, the bleachers would be full, and between the bleachers they had a microphone and microphone stand just for me to announce the games. That was one of the times I enjoyed high school. I was a real smart ass when the opposing team would be called for traveling, and I was on the mic saying, "he's walking everybody, caught in the act." Some nights the opposing team threatened to kill me.

One night stands out like a nightmare. I was walking into the school before that night's game, and my glasses fell. One of the lenses shattered when they hit the sidewalk. I wore my glasses to announce the game with one lens in and one gone. I could see clearly out of one eye, and the other was blurry. I don't know how I called that game. I wanted to play sports so bad and couldn't, and in my mind they didn't want me. I was really down about that. But when they asked me to announce the games that boosted my spirits. I felt wanted. I felt chosen.

I tried out for two school plays, and I was chosen for both. I was chosen, and they wanted me. I was already loving being on stage and performing. Although I went on to do standup for a band after graduating high school, I had no model of how to pursue that career. The closest city was Rochester, and I don't even know if they had a comedy club back in the early seventies.

My dad was the Chief of Police, and my uncle was a police officer for the Village of Geneseo. Day after day in my house, it was police talk. It was great fun to watch family and officers around the kitchen table laughing and telling stories. Some stories would be retold many times over, but the laughter and fun never stopped. And there were always new stories of arrests and incidents that had just happened. All I saw was that everybody loved their job. They loved talking about it and always had something different to talk about. So this was the model that was drawing me in. And my parents made it very clear as I approached graduation that I had a limited amount of time before I would have to leave the nest; there would be no failure to launch.

In my senior year, I took a criminal justice course that was taught at a trade school in Mt. Morris NY about fifteen miles from the high school. Once a week a bus would take us to the trade school. The course was taught by the Mt. Morris Chief of Police, Chuck Dipasquale. He had a big impact on me. I always remembered one day in class for the rest of my career. We were sitting in the police car for some type of police orientation. I was sitting in the driver's seat when I was put in a headlock. I remember it being severe. I remember choking for air and starting to panic. Just when it seemed I was going to pass out, I was released, and saw that my attacker was Chief Dipasquale. He very seriously said to me, "Don't ever let anyone sneak up on you like that, always be aware of your surroundings, or you will get yourself killed." For the next thirty-five years, I would always remember that when I sat in a police car. Chief Dipasquale was another supercop, just like dad.

5

It was during this trade school that I became good friends with Jim Chiverton. Jim introduced himself to me by saying, "Your father worked with my father at the Sheriff's Dept." My dad had worked with Jim's dad at the Livingston County Sheriff's Department years before my dad went to the Caledonia P.D. My dad said they were great friends, and Jim and I became great friends. After high school, we didn't keep in touch but would reunite some years later.

MONROE COMMUNITY COLLEGE

After high school I went to Monroe Community College in Henrietta just outside of Rochester NY. I enrolled in the Criminal Justice program. This was 1975, and MCC would gain some infamy as the college that Kenneth Bianchi attended in 1970. He later became known as one of the L.A. Hillside Stranglers. While going to the college, I worked part time as a security guard at Rochester General Hospital. My dad also helped me become a part time deputy Sheriff for the Livingston County Sheriff's Department, where he started his police career. While working as a volunteer I was able to attend a part time academy which was going to give our class full police officer certification by the New York State Bureau of Municipal Police.

Just short of two classes to complete my associates degree, I stopped going to MCC and focused on my uniformed ride alongs with the Livingston County Sheriff's Department headquartered in Geneseo NY. After a year of riding with several training deputies and having received my training certification, I was cleared to work by myself. I was still just twenty years old. This was quite thrilling. I had put in a lot of hours riding the night shift with other deputies. The only way to get hired by the Sheriff's Department was to be known by the Sheriff. At the time it was not a civil service job. The Sheriff decides who to hire. So the command staff and Sheriff have to like you, or you will not get hired. So volunteering as a part timer is equivalent to interning for a corporation.

HIRED FULL TIME

I want to reiterate the size of the Livingston County Sheriff's Department when I joined. About fifty total deputies made up of all divisions: road, jail, desk, civil and detective. There were twenty five road deputies (the deputies who worked strictly patrol). The jail had a maximum capacity of about fifty inmates. The jail population was about thirty when I started. The county was about 500 square miles and the population was about 60,000. On the midnight shift, we would normally have three patrol deputies working three different areas and a field sergeant. On the nights that we were shorthanded and had only two deputies, we would split the county in two with each deputy being responsible for half the county. The county is about 30 miles long and 20 miles wide. It would not be unusual to have a response time of thirty minutes to a call. And most calls, regardless of the type, would be handled by one deputy with no back up.

My first traffic stop working a one person car turned into a felony arrest. My first stop yielded me an arrest for Driving While Intoxicated (DWI) as opposed to Driving Under The Influence (DUI) in California. In New York at the time, your second arrest for DWI within five years of a previous conviction was a Felony. Unlike California where they use the preliminary hearing system to determine if a case should go to trial, N.Y uses the grand jury.

Still working part time, I was volunteering on a midnight shift. I made a traffic stop which resulted in an arrest for possession of marijuana. This was 1978 in upstate NY, so possession of any amount of marijuana was a felony. While I was at the station, I heard the sergeant yell to someone on the desk, "Call the Sheriff and let him know Yates made a drug arrest." The Sheriff had made a policy to be notified any time, day or night, whenever a deputy made a drug arrest. I thought to myself, The Sheriff is going to be losing sleep because I'm going to be hustling to make drug arrests. I was trying to get hired full time, and you have to make sure the Sheriff knows who you are. He knew who I was, but I wanted him to know I was out there on the night shift working and bringing people to the jail.

The same month I turned 21, August of 1978, I was offered a full time position with the Livingston County Sheriff's Department. Straight to patrol division. I worked with training officers, something like a week on each shift, and then I was sent out on my own on the midnight shift. I had already been putting in two to three shifts a week as a volunteer part time deputy, and now I was going to be getting paid. This was a very exciting time in my life. Now I was going to be paid for something I enjoyed doing for free.

First night working full time by myself on the midnight shift. I remember I had just pulled out of the Sheriff's Office driveway at 4 Court Street in Geneseo when I got my first call.

"111 MVA (motor vehicle accident) Route 63 just west of 36 car into a pole."

Lights and siren, I drove like a maniac and was first on the scene before fire and the ambulance arrived. It was a 1970's Volkswagen bug, and it was really smashed up against a telephone pole. It looked like the taillights were about two feet from the telephone pole. I came to learn that most late night traffic accidents on rural roads have that strange mix of sights and smells. There's an eerie quiet mixed with the sound of the police car engine and rotating emergency lights and the broken glass grinding under your feet as you approach the scene. The rotating lights bounce off the trees and shattered glass is strewn all over the roadway. The smell of gasoline and burning rubber mixes with the smells of the season. The summer smells could be freshly cut grass, wheat or corn. The winter smells could be fresh snow or dirty slush with salt and sand from the snow plows. Sometimes there is alcohol mixed in with it all.

As I approached the driver's door of the VW Bug, I saw the left side cheek and hair of a girl. About the width of five feet were the pole, windshield, steering wheel, girl's face, seat, and back of the car. All that was visible from outside the driver's window was a young woman's hair, left ear and cheek. The rest of her body was somewhere lost under the steering wheel which was against the front glass which was up against the telephone pole. As I leaned toward the young lady, I heard her moaning. I tried talking to her, but she could only respond with moaning. Over forty one years later and I can still remember the sound of her moaning. The fire department and ambulance arrived and were able to remove her with the jaws of life. She was transported to the hospital. I finished up the accident scene while another deputy responded to the hospital to check on the young lady. She had packed up her belongings from attending a summer program at S.U.N.Y Geneseo. She was on her way home to the Buffalo area when she apparently fell asleep at the wheel, drifted off the road and struck the telephone pole. I removed a set of golf clubs from the car before it was towed away.

A few minutes after the car had been towed away, I was notified that the young lady had been pronounced dead at the hospital. The next morning a very distraught dad came to the Sheriff's Office to pick up his deceased daughter's golf clubs. I was not at the station, but I was told the look of despair and grief on the dad's face was a very sad sight.

Working the midnight shift on back rural roads, I came to see too many fatal car accidents involving people who fell asleep at the wheel and hit a pole, tree or oncoming traffic. Whenever I have come close to being sleepy while driving, my brain floods with all these images and sounds of those fateful nights.

On another warm summer weekend night at about 2 am, I received an MVA call over the radio.

"109 a car into the guardrail on Route 5 and 20 in the town of Lima."

I arrived first on the scene, and it was a large white car that had been traveling east on Route 5 and 20 that had crossed the westbound lane and struck the guardrail, coming to rest. There was hardly any damage to the left driver's side of the car that hit the guardrail. As I approached the car, the fire and ambulance units were just arriving.

The lone male driver was unresponsive, but he did have some blood at the top of his head. They transported him to the hospital where he was pronounced dead on arrival. He was on his way home from work when he apparently fell asleep and drifted across the opposite lane of traffic. It was a very hot night and he had his driver's window open. When the left side of the car hit the guardrail, his head swung out the window and struck the guardrail, killing him instantly.

The accident was about five miles from his home. I finished the accident scene and then had the task of notifying the man's wife that her husband had been killed. The desk advised me that I would have to transport her to the hospital so she could make an identification. The desk had a local clergyman and a neighbor meet me at the door of the couple's house. She answered and I gave her the news. It's one of the worst things about our job. Such a sad, sad thing. I transported her to the Noyes Memorial Hospital in Dansville NY and I remember riding with her in the elevator down to the morgue of the hospital. It was just like you see on television. They pulled the body out of a compartment. As we stood at his head, the sight that stays with me is when she reached out and touched the cheek of her husband. That was a significant emotional event for me, and that memory comes to me from time to time, her reaching out and touching his cheek.

I will never fall asleep while driving.

FAMILY OF BLUE BLOODS

My dad was a cop starting his career with the Livingston County Sheriff's Department. He became the Chief of Police at the Village of Caledonia. He spent the last ten years of his career as a patrol officer and crime scene technician at the Greece NY. Police department.

My dad's brother and my uncle, Ted Yates, was a police officer for the Villa.ge of Geneseo Police Department. Not only was he an amazing cop, he also was a champion trap shooter. When I say champion, I mean champion. He garnered many titles and was inducted into the New York State trap shooters hall of fame.

While I was a deputy for the Livingston County Sheriff's Department my cousin Fred Yates, Ted's son, was a police officer for the village of Geneseo. Fred was also a legendary local softball player. Like Babe Ruth he would stand at the plate and point to the fence he was going to hit the homerun over. Fred and I bowled together on a league for many years. I may have gone on years later to get my PBA (Professional Bowlers Association) card and compete in professional events. But Fred was the better bowler, gathering numerous sanctioned 300 games.

When I left the Livingston County Sheriff's Department for California, I was twenty six years old. Another of Ted's boys who was also my cousin, Sherman Yates, was about sixteen. A few years later and Sherman would join the Livingston County Sheriff's Department. Sherman left Livingston County to be the Chief of Police for the Mt. Morris Police Department. Sherman left Mt. Morris for the Palmyra NY. Police Department where he rose to the rank of Chief.

On my dad's side, we had quite a tradition of policing.

FRIENDS REUNITED

I was working the day shift for some unknown reason. It must have been an overtime shift. I hated the day shift. I continued to hate the day shift throughout my 35 years in Law Enforcement. I love the midnight shift: 12 midnight until 8 in the morning. But here I was working the day shift, and I received some type of report call at a car dealership in Avon N.Y. When I arrived I was met by one of the car salesmen, Jim Chiverton. I told you about Jim from my high school Criminal Justice class who I had lost touch with after high school. While I was going to Monroe Community College for Criminal Justice, Jim had gone into the service and worked as an MP. He caught me up on his world travels. I remember he had great stories and fond memories from his time in the Azores. Jim said he wasn't happy working as a salesman for the car dealership. He said that I was living the dream, and there would be nothing he would like more than working full time as a Livingston County Sheriff's Deputy. He thought it would be great if he and I could work together at the Sheriff's Department like our dads.

I arranged for him to go on a ride along with me on the night shift. We had a great time on our shift, and he was more determined than ever to become a full time deputy. I encouraged him to follow the path I did by starting part time, learning the ropes and getting to know the Sheriff so when a full time opening came up, he would be at the top of the list. Jim did get hired part time, and I was able to train him on the midnight shift. Shortly thereafter, Jim realized his dream of becoming a full time Livingston County Sheriff's Deputy.

One afternoon shift I was working alone driving south on Route 15 at a high speed. Up ahead I saw a large black cloud over the road. Just before I reached the cloud, I realized it was a swarm of bees. I was able to maintain my speed as I leaned over to the passenger door with my left hand on the steering wheel while I rolled the window up with my right hand. I got the window up just as my police cruiser slammed into the swarm of bees. I turned around and drove back toward the swarm and saw the hive boxes on the west side of the road. Yes, this was before the days of power windows, when you had to actually crank the windows by hand.

A few nights later, Jim and I were working together. It was about two in the morning. I had forgotten about the bee incident until we drove by the hive boxes. I didn't say anything, but Jim said, "Hey, what are those colored boxes we just passed?"

I knew what they were, but I didn't tell Jim. I just said, "Let's go back and take a look." I did a couple U-turns and stopped on the side of the road about thirty feet from the boxes.

Jim got out and walked up to the boxes. As he got close to the hive boxes, I hit the siren a couple times. The siren must have got those bees a buzzing, because all of a sudden Jim was in a full sprint back toward the Sheriff's car. Jim was not gaining any ground on our patrol car, as I had put it in reverse and was backing up at about the same pace that Jim was running. I know, that was mean. Well, I had to make sure he wasn't going to be bringing a swarm of bees into the car with him. I only let him run about a hundred yards before I stopped, and he jumped into the car. I found out he had as big a fear of bees as I had. He was so happy to be safely in the car, he couldn't even be mad at me.

I was laughing so hard, I had tears rolling down my face, and Jim soon joined in, and it was a while before we both could stop laughing. Jim was usually the one playing the jokes on other deputies, so I was happy to get one in on him. Jim was the kind of guy that enjoyed the joke even if it was played on him. He just enjoyed life and enjoyed laughing. We had a great time working together on the midnight shift over the next four years. For a time my friend and roommate Larry Tetamore, Jim and I were the core of the midnight shift. Sometimes after our shift was over we would all get breakfast together and then go over to Jim's and listen to music. I remember one morning Jim couldn't wait to show us a music video on MTV from Meat Loaf, "Bat out of Hell." I can't hear that song without thinking of that morning we all spent together.

In 1983 I left Livingston County to join the Los Angeles County Sheriff's Department. On occasion I would stop by and visit my deputy friends at the Livingston County Sheriff's Office when I was home. Over the next few years, my visits were more infrequent, and I lost touch with my Livingston County family. I'll get to that part of the story a little later.

In 1987, Jim had a case where one of the witnesses had not been served a subpoena. The witness was crucial to Jim's case, and the case was about to start trial. The court division had been unable to serve the witness. Jim was so dedicated to his job, he decided to serve the subpoena himself. He had to drive to the Rochester, NY area, which is about twenty miles north of Livingston County. Jim was driving north on Route 390 near Henrietta NY when he was hit head on by a car traveling south in the northbound lanes of the expressway.

Off-duty Monroe County Sheriff's Sergeant Tom Vasile was driving north on Route 390. When he noticed traffic was stopped, he got out of his car and saw it was a traffic accident. Tom was good friends with both Jim and I. Tom walked toward the crash scene, and had no idea he would be seeing Jim trapped in the crashed car. Jim did not survive the crash. The other driver was an elderly man, who also did not survive.

Tom went with the other officers to make the death notification to the family of the elderly driver that struck Jim's car. Tom said when they knocked, the man's daughter opened the door, and the first thing she said was, "Please don't tell me he killed anyone." She went on to tell the officers that she had been trying for a long time to get her father's driver's license taken away. She said he was getting confused and in her opinion should not be driving. She feared that he would get confused, and do something like enter the expressway going the wrong way, and kill himself and someone else. Which is exactly what happened. Rest in peace, Jim Chiverton. Please go to the Officer Down Memorial Page and read about Jim.

Tom Vasile is one of my best friends. When my dad was Chief of Police in Caledonia, he had hired Tom as a police officer. That was Tom's first police job. Some nights Tom would be working the Village of Caledonia and Larry, Jim and I would be working the county cars.

So, we all became good friends. It was a weird twist of fate that years later Tom would stop at the accident scene on Route 390 where he would find Jim dead.

CONESUS DRIVE IN

It seems most of my memories are of incidents that happened on warm summer nights. I was working the east side of the county one warm summer night. When you worked the east car on a weekend night, you knew you were probably in for a busy night. Conesus Lake, one of the finger lakes, is in east area which has several restaurants and bars along its shores. There is a drive-in which back in the 1970's and early 80's was really hopping on the weekends.

It was about 1 am when I received a call to respond to the drive-in along with fire and an ambulance, and they didn't give me any other details. I pulled into the drive-in and it was a weird scene. There was nothing showing on the screen, all the lights were on, and the drive-in was still packed. Groups of people were outside their cars, and there was no noise. All the cars were in the position they were in while they were watching the movie, except for one car that was in the roadway area between the rows of cars. There was a large group gathered around that car in the roadway, so I drove right up to it. The front of my police car was facing the front of the car. When I stepped out of my patrol car, a lady ran up to me and grabbed my arms yelling, "I killed him, I killed the boy, the little boy is dead!"

The ambulance people arrived, and they took the lady to their ambulance to try and calm her down. I walked to a group of people who were gathered at the rear of the brown car in the roadway. They directed me to the left rear tire of the car, and someone pointed toward the rear tire saying, "He's under the car, deputy." I got down lying flat on my stomach and started crawling in the dirt with my flashlight under the car. As I got under the car and started shining my light, I saw that a little boy was severely mangled in the rear end universal joint of the car. His head and shoulders were wedged up on top the of universal joint. Closest to me was his left arm and hand laying down in the dirt, palm up. I grabbed his wrist to feel for a pulse, and I remember his watch coming off, and I put it in my pocket. I don't know why I grabbed his wrist for a pulse; he was so badly mangled it was obvious that he was dead.

He turned out to be a 12 year old boy from Pennsylvania visiting friends on his summer vacation. I think a part of me was in shock of this scene like everyone else. No time for that. On this night I couldn't be like everyone else, I was the cop who had to make decisions and get things that needed to happen going. This one took a little bit to piece together.

The boy was staying with a family in the area when they decided to go to the drive-in. I remember they had a van. It was a couple, their three children and the visiting boy. They invited a neighbor lady, a single mom and her two boys to go to the drive-in also. The couple and their three with the visiting boy drove in their van while the neighbor and her two boys went in a different car. They arrived at the drive-in and parked side by side so the kids could hang out during the movie.

One of the neighbor lady's boys and the visiting boy laid down in front of her brown car on blankets during the movie. When the movie ended, the neighbor lady's two boys got into the car. The kids and couple in the van were gathering their things. The lady said her goodbye and pulled out of the spot over the hump, turning left. As she slowly drove along the roadway for about one hundred feet, a lady was running alongside of her car banging on the driver's window yelling, "You ran over a boy! You ran over a boy!" The neighbor lady immediately stopped the car and got out. She looked under the car, and seeing the boy started running and screaming.

When her two boys got into her car, she didn't know that the visiting boy was still asleep on the blanket in front of her car. As she pulled out, she ran over top of him. As her car went over the hump of the drive-in space, she mangled him in the universal joint of the car and dragged him under until she was stopped by the lady pounding on her driver's window. Her boy got up when the movie ended and didn't realize that the visiting boy was still asleep.

I handled the investigation, towing of the car, interviewing of the witnesses and writing the report. No other cars showed up for assistance, which was not unusual. It just seems weird when I look back after joining the L.A. Sheriff's Department. A similar call in L.A would have commanded a response of probably four or five cars back up, and at least one supervisor. There would have been homicide detectives even though it was an accident and crime scene technicians.

But this was Livingston County in 1978, things were different. As our Sheriff in Livingston county once said, one call one deputy.

I remember going back to the Sheriff's Office to call the Pennsylvania State Police to make the death notification to the boys' parents. While on the phone, I remembered the watch and pulled it from my left front pants pocket. I still see that black watch with the LED display and the broken band on the desk in front of me as I was on the phone talking to a Pennsylvania State Trooper.

CRAZY WAS GOING TO SHOOT ME

One night at about 1 am I was patrolling the north end, traveling west on Route 5 and 20 between East Avon and the Village of Avon. I saw a car traveling toward me east weaving across the center lines of the road. When I made a U-turn, the chase was on. I radioed that I was in a high-speed chase. We got up to 100 mph when the car turned its lights out and turned right into a strip mall in East Avon. When I turned into the driveway of the large parking lot, I saw the car slowly moving forward with the driver's door open. Out of the corner of my eye, I saw a person running from the parking lot into some backyards.

The car came to a stop at the corner of the empty parking lot. I looked inside and saw there was nobody else in the car. I ran to where I last saw the person running. I went around the corner of a large shed and couldn't see anything. I tried a bluff, pointing my gun toward some bushes I yelled, "Come out, or I'll blow your fucking head off!"

About ten yards from me, a male came out from behind a tree with his hands up and said, "Ok, I give up." I ordered him down on the ground where I handcuffed him. He was extremely intoxicated, and I arrested him for Driving While Intoxicated.

By the time I got him back to my Sheriff's car, some backup units had arrived. I transported my arrest to Geneseo to the Sheriff's Office where he submitted to a breathalyzer, the result being a .17. At that time in NY .10 was the legal limit. I had the desk call the local justice and had him meet me at the Avon town hall so I could arraign my prisoner. Years later when I got to California, I would be working in a system with a bail schedule which is already set, and there was no arraignment prior to transporting to a custody facility, but in New York these were justice courts where you arraigned all arrests, and if bail could not be met, the Judge issued a commitment to the jail. The Judge was usually not a judge in the truest sense. They were justices who heard misdemeanor and traffic cases. In this case on this night, the justice was a local dairy farmer by trade, and being a justice was the side job. Several times I had to transport my prisoner to the farm and have the justice arraign my prisoner at the dairy farm. Some of these justices had offices at their home to conduct arraignments.

When I walked into the court section of the town hall, my prisoner's mother was already there. The Judge (town justice, but we called them Judge) released my prisoner on his own recognizance and gave him a court date. I had a fit and let the Judge know that I was pissed off and that this drunk that ran from me should have bail set, and he should be locked up. My prisoner, by the way, was not cooperative and kind of a wingnut. In my opinion, his mother was not going to be able to take control of him in his current condition. The Judge told me bail was not punishment but meant to secure his appearance in court, and since his mother was present and willing to take responsibility for her son, the best decision was to release him to his mother. I was a 23-year-old hard ass who basically felt that if you're driving drunk and then you lead the police on a chase and then you flee on foot, you should have your ass kicked at least, and then definitely be locked up. The Judge let me know that I was not the Judge.

I left the town hall and drove to the Star Diner right in the Village of Avon to have breakfast. By now it was 4 am, and I was hungry. I ordered my usual five eggs over easy with toast and coffee. The waitress said to me, "I heard you arrested Crazy." I told her I didn't know that was his nickname, but it sure fits. I guess because I was mad about the judge not sending Crazy to jail I stayed in the diner longer than normal. Instead of finishing my breakfast and leaving, I stayed in the booth by the door, having a couple more cups of coffee and starting my police report. I was probably in the diner for about 45 minutes. When the waitress brought my check, she looked out the front window and said, "There's Crazy's truck, and his mom is out there too."

I walked outside, and Crazy's mom was pounding on the driver's window of a pickup truck parked parallel to the front of the diner. "You better not let him drive," I said, getting into my police car. I drove back down to the town hall and got on a payphone in front of the building and called the Judge at his house. I was yelling at him, "You let that Crazy go, you know where he is now? He is in a pickup in front of the Star Diner with his mom pounding on his truck window. He obviously drove there—he could have killed someone, and you're the one who let him out." Before I could finish my tirade, to my dismay I saw Crazy drive right past me, looking at me with a crazy look. I just hung up on the Judge and jumped in my police car and gave chase of Crazy. Surprisingly, Crazy pulled over right away.

When I approached the driver's door, he was pounding on the steering with both fists yelling, "You mother fucker I will kill you!" He ignored my commands and kept yelling and pounding on the steering wheel. I went back to the police car and radioed for back up. It was now past 5 am. All the village police cars had gone off duty, and my nearest Sheriff unit was 20 minutes away. But an off duty New York State Trooper who had a take home car heard my call for back up on his home monitor. He lived just down the street from where I was and was just getting up to start his shift. He responded, and when Crazy saw the two of us, he exited the truck, and I arrested him for Driving While Intoxicated for the second time of the same day. The trooper said he would stay with the truck until a Sheriff's unit arrived to handle the towing of the truck.

I transported my prisoner back to the Sheriff's Office for a second breathalyzer test, this time he blew a .10. While I was at the station processing my arrest, my assisting unit radioed to advise me that he found a loaded 12 gauge shotgun under the seat of the pickup truck, so I added the charge of carrying a loaded shotgun in a vehicle. Yes, we went back to the same old judge for another arraignment. This time there was to be no release without bail, and if I remember right, the bail was quite high. Off to jail went Crazy. That was the last I thought or heard of Crazy for about two weeks.

I had just started my midnight shift when I got a call on the Sheriff's radio.

"101 to 111."

101—holy shit, that was the call number for the Sheriff himself. The previous Sheriff had the call sign of 100. He died in office of a heart attack, so they retired that call sign. The new Sheriff, Dick Kane, became 101. So 101 called me on the radio and told me to meet him at his house. This was highly unusual. I was thinking, What did I do now? Everyone else in the county heard the call on the radio and were probably wondering the same thing.

I got to the Sheriff's house, and he said, "Remember that guy in Avon you arrested for DWI, and he had the shotgun under the front seat?"

I said, "Crazy? Yeah, I remember. He is a real asshole."

"Well, a jail informant told one of the detectives he was in a cell with Crazy, and Crazy told him he had been arrested for drunk driving and when he was released, he went home and got his shotgun with the intent of shooting the deputy that arrested him. He loaded his shotgun and drove to the Star Diner because he knew that's where the deputies would go to eat. When he got to the diner, he saw the Sheriff's car, so he parked parallel to the front so when the deputy came out he could shoot him as he walked out the door. But the deputy was in the diner so long he fell asleep. When he woke up, his mother was pounding on his truck window. When he saw the Sheriff's car gone, he went driving into town looking for the deputy, but got pulled over and couldn't get the drop on him. So, Crazy got out of jail today, and I wanted to make sure somebody told you about this so you would be careful."

I thanked the Sheriff and told him not to worry; I would be careful. Now it all fell together why Crazy was outside the Star Diner, and his mom was pounding on the window. Crazy ended up taking a plea deal and did some time. I can't remember where or for how long. I continued to work in that area from time to time, but never saw Crazy again. This is one of a few times, but for the grace of God, I was not killed. Sometimes I think to myself, Wow, that was crazy. Pun intended.

DRIVING TOO FAST TO GET SHOT

I was directed by the dispatcher to drive into the Rochester Police Department and pick up a prisoner at the lockup and transport him back to the Livingston County Jail. It's 30 miles from the Sheriff's Office to the Rochester Police Department. I was in the town of Avon when I got the call patrolling for an arrest. It was about 3 am, prime time for making an arrest or for getting into a chase. This kind of call pissed me off, it took me out of the game.

I picked up my prisoner from the Rochester jail and was headed back to Geneseo to drop him off at our jail. I was screaming south on Route 15 approaching Livingston County. I was doing about 90 when I saw a man hitchhiking along the right shoulder of the road. I always stopped to check out hitchhikers. Often they were wanted felons, had just committed a crime, possessed weapons or were under the influence of drugs. As soon as my headlights hit the hitchhiker his big round face looked weird. I jumped on the brakes hard so I could stop and check him out. I knew I shouldn't with a prisoner in the back, but I was rogue. I was going so fast by the time I got slowed to make a stop I was a hundred yards past the hitchhiker. I remember saying fuck it, and got right back on the accelerator and continued south on Route 15. My prisoner said, "That was a weird looking fucker."

I dropped off my prisoner and went into the dispatch office to shoot the shit with the desk. I told them I had passed a mongoloid looking guy on Route 15 but couldn't stop to check him out.

Later in the afternoon, one of our detectives came to my house. He asked me if I remembered driving by a guy hitchhiking about 3 am on Route 15. He then showed me a six pack (a group of similar looking mug type pictures used in identifying suspects). I picked out the guy right away. The hitchhiker had down's syndrome. At the time of the incident, it was common to use the term mongoloid. The history dates back to when Mongolia was discovered and people with down's syndrome were incorrectly thought to look like people from Mongolia. It has since become a politically incorrect term.

The detective told me that prior to my driving by him he had been hitchhiking on Route 15 in Henrietta (just outside of Rochester NY), and a woman picked him up. He shot the woman in the face with a handgun, pushed her out of the car and took her car. The car stopped running, so he got out and started hitchhiking again, and a short time later we drove past him. When they picked him up still hitchhiking later that morning, he had the gun in his possession with one bullet left in it. He said the guy admitted shooting the woman and stated, "If that cop that started to stop had tried to arrest me, I was going to shoot him too."

Full disclosure, I have to humbly admit during these early years—during this incident and the crazy shotgun incident—I was not at all the epitome of officer safety. It was no credit to my tactics that I had survived some harrowing encounters up to this point in my police career. Looking back, I'm sure God or his angels were looking out for me. I wasn't even wearing a bulletproof vest at this point. This incident with the mongoloid hitchhiker got my attention because I knew at the time my intention was to quickly stop with my prisoner and talk to the hitchhiker through the passenger window and make my initial inquiry as to what he was doing. About the laziest, poorest and most dangerous way of making a contact. Another day through my own ignorance and lack of tactics could have gotten myself killed. But, a chance friendship was about to change that in a big way.

THE AMAZING DAVE FASANO

It was about 3 am on a Sunday morning. I was in the Village of Geneseo just driving out of the Sheriff's Office parking lot at 4 Court Street when I heard on the radio a call for back up from a Leroy Police Officer. Leroy was a small village 23 miles away from Geneseo in a neighboring county, so I didn't pay too much attention. When the second or third back up request came out where the officer reported that he was holding burglary suspects at gunpoint and no one was answering, fuck that, I got on the radio and advised I was responding. A part of me thought that out of embarrassment closer units would start responding before I could get there.

I was rolling hard, lights and siren were both on and I was driving much faster than would be considered reasonable. These were two-lane roads in rural Livingston County at 3 am with little or no traffic. Between the small villages of Avon and Caledonia and Leroy, I was able to hit 100 plus miles per hour most of the way. No other units ever did respond. I was the only backup car to arrive. I'm sure it was longer, but it seemed like I made it in five minutes.

As I arrived on Route 5 a mile or two east of the Village of Leroy, I saw the car stop. The car was facing east on the shoulder with the Leroy Police Car just behind it offset with rotating lights flashing. Car keys were in the middle of the street, and several males were lying face down with their arms outstretched. I heard the officer's voice from the vehicle loudspeaker barking commands to the other occupants of the car. I did a U-turn and parked behind the Leroy Police Car which had both front car doors open. I walked up to the passenger side door and leaned in to talk to the officer. The police car was empty. Then a voice from behind a tree about 10 yards south of the police car said, "I'm over here, handcuff those guys while I cover you." I was thinking, What the fuck? I just heard you barking commands from the front loudspeaker of your patrol car.

This was my introduction to my lifelong friend, the amazing Dave Fasano. I was really interested in this whole takedown scenario. Dave later asked me, "Haven't you been to a street survival seminar by Calibre Press?" I said no, and he said he would take care of that. Dave had conducted a felony stop not by the book, but beyond the book into ninja street survival tactics. Dave explained how he had opened both doors so the suspects would believe there were two officers. He switched his radio to broadcast over the car's loudspeaker, so when he issued commands it would sound as if he was using the cars PA system and not safely away from the car on his handheld radio. If the suspects had started shooting into the police car, they would be shooting into an empty car, and it would not have ended good for them.

Dave and I are the best of friends to this day. I think I had a special place in Dave's heart from day one because he knew I went balls out to back him up coming from such a great distance. We were of similar mindsets. Some might describe us as crazy fuckers.

Dave and I attended a couple of street survival seminars together. To me, Dave was an amazing street cop and remains an amazing loyal friend to this day. Dave had always wanted to be a police officer. To be a cop in NY, you had to be 20. Dave couldn't wait and took a job as a police officer in Key West Florida at age 18. Dave became a police officer in Key West at age 18, and not working the desk, or in the jail. He started right on the street. Dave worked Key West for two years. Dave is a private guy, and I will leave his stories for him to tell. But you can imagine Key West in the '70s. Night Clubs, Big Drugs, Big Money, Big Crime. Dave had big-time police stories which fed into my growing dream of joining a big city law enforcement agency. A dream that had been growing since I started reading police books about Los Angeles and New York City.

BLEEDING HOUSE

I was patrolling the north end on a freezing winter night driving through the Village of Caledonia when I got the call to meet the informant of a domestic violence call in Dansville, a village about 30 miles south of where I was in Caledonia. This is one of those nights we were running short, and two of us were splitting the county. My area was Caledonia to the north and Dansville, Nunda to the south. I met the young man who made the call at the Truck Stops of America in Dansville. He said that earlier in the day his girlfriend and her ex-husband had a custody hearing regarding their three your old daughter. Tonight he was visiting his girlfriend in the house that she and her daughter live in located in the Town of Sparta.

The ex-husband showed up at the house, and while in the front foyer, they got involved in a physical struggle. The ex grabbed a handful of shotgun shells from a box on the key table in the foyer. The ex then left the home and started walking up the road to his parents' house. He returned to the front door a few minutes later, holding a shotgun. The informant went on to say that he believed the ex was going to shoot him, so he ran from the back door to the driveway and got into his corvette. As he backed out of the driveway, he heard two shotgun blasts. When he got to a safe location, he saw that the side of his car had been hit with shotgun pellets.

I remember the informant saying to me, "Please, deputy. We have to get to the house. I think he will hurt her. She is not answering the phone, and he might kill her."

I called the desk and talked to the field sergeant, Kent Waltman. He said he and some backup units would meet me at the house. Sergeant Waltman, Detectives Smith and York, and another backup unit met me at the house in Sparta. This house was out in the middle of nowhere. It was a very cold wintery night and snowing hard. Another deputy and I took cover in the backyard while the detectives and Sergeant Waltman went to the front. I remember being in the backyard for what seemed like a long time. Finally, we were called to the front door.

They had gotten no response by telephone and banging on the

door. When I got to the front, the three-year-old girl opened the door. I remember Detective York picking up the little girl and asking her, "Are Mommy and Daddy home?" The little girl shook her head yes but didn't say anything. This was a large A-frame house. I found out later the husband had built it. Detective York asked the little girl, "Are Mommy and Daddy upstairs?" The little girl again nodded her head yes.

Sergeant Waltman said, "Let's go, we have to go get up there."

Waltman started up the stairs, and Detective York whispered, "Kent, you don't have a vest on."

Waltman turned to York. "I don't need a fucking vest," he said before he started back up the stairs.

We were all in a row: Waltman, Detectives York and Smith, myself and another deputy. We had gone up about three steps when Waltman stopped and put his flashlight on the walls of the stairway. He had felt that the railing was wet. When he turned on his light, we saw blood was dripping down the walls of the stairway from the top floor. Sergeant Waltman continued to the top of the stairs and was first to walk around a corner and out of sight. He quickly returned with his gun back in his holster, and he spoke in a normal tone of voice. "They're both up here."

And they were both in the bathroom. The door was off its hinges. She was shot in the face, laying on her back in the corner between the wall and toilet. His back and shoulders were leaned back against the tub with most of the top of his head gone, and his brain was in the bathtub. After shooting at the boyfriend who was backing out of the driveway in his corvette, the ex-husband had continued into the house and chased his ex-wife up the stairs. She shut and locked the bathroom door. He kicked the door off of its hinges. She cowered in the rear of the bathroom, trying to shield her face with her arms. He shot her in the face at close range, killing her instantly. He then put the gun to the side of his head and blew the top of his head off, and his brain landed in the bathtub. He fell to the floor against the tub with the gun lying on top of him. The blood had poured out of the bathroom and down onto the stairwell.

The little girl must have been standing in the doorway or close by when this happened because later they found she had three pieces of birdshot from the shotgun blast in her leg. After the bodies had been taken away, I was to stay behind and wait for one of our crime scene technicians, which was a full-time deputy wearing two hats. Before everyone else left, Detective York told me to go back upstairs and close a window in the bedroom. When I went upstairs and went into the bedroom, it was an eerie feeling seeing their wedding and family pictures on the dresser. And now two parents were dead, and their three-year-old daughter was left behind.

The dispatcher who was on the night of the call would later purchase this house. I told him that I could not imagine living in that house after seeing such a gruesome scene. He told me years later that the toilet had sprung a leak, and water had leaked into the floor and came out onto the stairway. It was red from the blood that had soaked in years before, the night of the shooting. That's when I named it the bleeding house.

HELLS ANGELS MEETIING

I was working the west side, and I got a loud music call deep in the woods of the town of Nunda. At the time, I was talking to a New York State Trooper. I told the trooper I had to go on this noise complaint deep in the woods. He told me they were having a Hells Angels National meeting there, and it probably was not a good idea to go.

Mainly because I'm an idiot, I said, "Fuck that, I'm going."

The trooper said he knew the head guy and would go with me to make contact. We got to this back road location, and there were probably over two hundred motorcycles and more cars and trucks than that. We had to walk what seemed like a mile into the woods where the trooper and I strolled into a group of over five hundred members of the outlaw motorcycle gang Hells Angels who were gathered around a large bonfire. Thank God the trooper was with me; he knew who to ask for. He told the head guy some local had called in a complaint about the music, so we were obligated to respond.

The head guy said, "Thanks for coming, I'll make sure we keep the noise down," and was kind of smirking.

We said thank you and promptly left—two against these 500 bikers, what the fuck were we going to do. The nearest house was probably two miles away. This was probably the best place for them to have their meeting. As we walked down the dirt road to our police cars, I looked into some of the cars parked along the shoulder. I saw police uniform patches, police batons, and handguns on the seats. We were out of there. I shouldn't even have gone on that call. That's the kind of call you went on by yourself on the back roads of Livingston County.

The kind of town Nunda was, there was a bar called the Hogs' Trough. Two Hatfield brothers, yes Hatfield like Hatfield and McCoys, were kicked out of the Hogs' Trough. They went home and returned to the bar with a chainsaw and promptly sawed the bar in half. Those same brothers later tied up a couple in their home and then set it on fire, killing them both. The Hatfields are in Attica State Prison now doing life. That was the mentality in some of those backwoods communities. As a Livingston County Sheriff's Deputy, you would respond to these type of calls yourself with backup about 25 minutes away. We didn't have handheld radios. We had pagers. So if the desk needed help, they could get ahold of us, but we were shit out of luck.

MY ANKLE BROKE

One weekend night I was working radar in the Village of Livonia. I was monitoring traffic traveling east on Route 20A into the 30 mph zone. A red Chevy Nova came into town, and the radar gun flashed 62. As I pulled on to the roadway and put on my overhead lights, the Nova took off, and the chase was on. The Nova fishtailed as it made a right turn onto Commercial Street and then made two more quick right turns on Big Tree Street and then Livonia Station. As the Nova slowed, the driver's door opened, and a mountain of a man jumped out of the car wearing a red and black checkered coat. I forgot to mention it was the middle of winter, and it was a cold night. There were piles of snow everywhere from recent plowing. The side streets were still covered in snow and ice.

I radioed that I was in foot pursuit and jumped out of my police car. I was a good 25 yards behind as we ran across Route 20A and then on to Grove Street. Grove Street immediately sloped steeply down. At the bottom of the slope, my fleeing suspect turned left in an alley. As I slid to a stop in my slick bottomed police shoes, my right ankle caught on some bare road, and I heard the crack of my right ankle. I couldn't walk on it and had to be driven back to my police car by a good Samaritan.

The car was not stolen and was registered to a well-known criminal. I'll call him Sampson. Detectives later told me that Sampson had a lengthy arrest record for resisting arrest and assault on peace officers, and it might have been a good thing I didn't catch him. He had a previous conviction for Driving While Intoxicated and was probably drunk again and didn't want to go down for the Felony. I did identify him from a six-pack, and he was arrested for Obstructing a peace officer and resisting arrest. He later pled to a lesser crime and did time in our county jail. My ankle was broken, and it was a long six-week recovery.

STOLEN CAR

Now in Livingston County, the pursuit policy was "they run, we chase." I don't think we had a pursuit policy. When I got to the Los Angeles County Sheriff's Department, the pursuit policy was pages thick. If you did the right 20 things in the right order at the right time, you might be allowed to continue a pursuit. But in 1979 in Livingston County, it was you run and we chase you until the wheels fall off.

On one of those late nights when another deputy and I were splitting the county, I was driving in the village of Geneseo trying to stay centrally located for calls. It was 3 am, and the dispatcher gave me a call in the village of Nunda of a car squealing tires. A village 30 miles away had someone squealing tires in the center of town, and they dispatched me for that. I was pissed off. When the bars let out, this happened all over the county. I knew by the time I got there 30 minutes later the streets would be bare, except for the rubber on the road from the squealing tires bandit.

I made it down to the village of Nunda, and as I suspected the village was a ghost town. Every bar was closed and not a car to be seen. For five minutes, I drove around town. I didn't want to leave too quickly and return to the center of the county in case my squealing tires culprit was still in the area.

About five minutes later on a side street, I saw taillights. I quickly got behind the pickup truck and stopped behind it at a stop sign. I turned on my overhead lights, and now I heard squealing tires, and the truck accelerated to over 80 mph on a side street. I broadcasted that I was in pursuit. There wasn't much purpose in announcing my pursuit because there were no police cars available to back me up within 20 miles. He made several turns on to back dirt roads with no street signs. The dispatcher who lives in the area was telling me where I was. I remember the dispatcher saying things like, "You're on county road one, and you should see a red barn with two silos on your right." This was like one of those back road chases you see on tv with dirt kicking up into my windshield as we drove close to 100 mph on this dirt road with deep ruts.

Suddenly he skidded to about 20 mph and turned into the right ditch, coming to a stop. The male driver jumped out of the truck and ran to the middle of a field of deep grass. I radioed I was in foot pursuit and trained my spotlight to where I last saw the suspect running and disappear in the grass. I ran to the middle of the field but didn't see the suspect. The field was too big and wide open for him to have made it to the woods nearby. I pulled out my gun. Time for my ruse again, yelling, "Stand the fuck up before I start peppering this field with bullets!"

He stood up about twenty feet from me. I was two for two on this one. This young guy had stolen the pickup an hour before I pulled up behind him at the stop sign. He was unarmed when I arrested him, and I found no weapon in the truck or in and around the field where I arrested him. I'm adding the no weapon information because one year later the same guy stole another car in the same area and was chased by a New York State Trooper, and again he ditched the stolen car and ran into the woods near the field where I had arrested him. This time when the trooper approached him, he raised a handgun pointing at the trooper. The trooper shot and killed him.

CAR DEER ACCIDENTS

Driving the open back roads on the midnight shift, you get used to driving at 100 mph going call to call. A detective used to tell us on the midnight shift, "Familiarity breeds contempt; slow down." His words would come to me on occasion, and I would slow down. One of the biggest fears we had was hitting a deer at high speed. It was not uncommon for us to respond to fatal car crashes involving car-deer accidents where the deer goes through the front windshield killing the driver. We had fatal accidents with cows and horses. Funny as it may seem, that was a common call on the night shift. Cows out in the road. We had so many smashed up police cars from deer accidents that the Sheriff put on what we called deer chasers on the bumpers of the patrol cars. The wind goes through a hole in them, causing an ultrasonic sound that supposedly the deer hear and stop running before they can leap into the path of the car. The first night Deputy Jim Chiverton drove a car with the deer chasers on, he hit a deer. That was the end of those.

Between October and December when the deer are rutting, and when deer season starts, the deer start moving around like crazy. Starting in late September, the car deer accidents would start. We had deer tags to issue to drivers who wanted to take the deer with them after the accident if they wanted. I hated that time of year because in many cases the deer would still be alive with maybe a couple of broken legs and have to be put down. Deer have a very small brain, so we would have to get real close and put a shot at the center of their heads to make sure they died. It was a sad thing when it was an afternoon and traffic was going by with kids watching this deer with one or two broken legs trying to hobble down an embankment to a field and escape. And we have to get to the deer and kill them before they get into a field out of sight and suffer. I probably put down over 20 deer in the five years I worked for the Livingston County Sheriff's Department.

There was a time before there were regulations and rules regarding the preparation of food for the jail inmates when you could bring dead deer from the accidents back to the jail. Deputies would bring the deer back to the Sheriff's Office to be hung in the Sheriff's garage while inmate trustees gutted them and prepared the venison to be served to the jail inmates. It was quite a sight to drive into the Sheriff's Office driveway and see deer hanging and trustees skinning them. The jail kitchen was quite a place, and the inmates were very happy to be eating fresh venison.

STORE ROBBERY

One of my days off in 1981, I drank too much. Oh my, did I drink too much, and I had a dayshift overtime spot to work. My drinking involved a function with numerous department members, and calling in sick would have been a bad move. I dragged myself out of bed with the pounding headache a hangover is happy to provide. I was working the 8 am to 4 pm shift and thinking, If I can just make it through this shift... I stopped at a friend's house in the east side area I was working midway through my shift and got my second dose of aspirin. I had a couple of report calls, and by 2 pm, I was feeling functional.

It was 2:40 pm when I got the call of an armed robbery in progress at the Millpond grocery in Springwater, one male with a shotgun. I remember saying out loud, "What the fuck." I have previously described the kind of calls we normally got. Car accidents, suicides, burglaries, high-speed chases, domestic calls. Robberies, not very often. Springwater was at the very south end of the east side. I started hauling ass, partly because it was a robbery in progress, and partly because I got off at 4 pm, and I was half expecting them to cancel the call and say it wasn't a robbery.

I was just south of Conesus on Route 15 when I saw a motorcycle coming toward me at a high rate of speed. As it passed me, I saw behind the driver the barrel of a shotgun sticking straight up in the air. I turned around, and the chase was on. I saw the shotgun barrel sticking out of one of those square plastic milk crates that was on the back of his motorcycle. I broadcasted my pursuit of the robbery suspect who made a right turn on to railroad avenue in the town of Conesus. This little back road was beginning to narrow, and I knew there was a hairpin turn coming up, and past that he had a good chance of losing me on a small service road. So as we reached the curve, I rammed the back of his motorcycle with my front bumper. This sent him through the curve in the road and into a ditch. He flew off the motorcycle, and I jumped out and was able to arrest him, recover the shotgun and $179 he stole from the small grocery store on Mill Street Extension in the Village of Springwater. Headache was gone.

IT'S SNOWING AND COLD

One night they gave me my assigned car. I walked out the back door of the Sheriff's Office where the patrol cars were parked. My assigned car had not been driven in a while as it had a foot of snow on it. I took a big push-broom and started pushing the snow off the hood. As I drew the broom back across the roof of the car, I pulled a shit load of snow onto and into my shoes. We all had to wear the same brand of shoes. And the brand of shoes we were wearing were open around the ankle, just enough to let snow fill down in around your ankle. They gave me an accident call as I was trying to clear my car off.

As I got in the frozen car, I had to wait for the defroster to create an ever-widening small hole in the ice-packed on my windshield. I was freezing in my patrol car, leaning forward peering out a hole in the ice above my steering wheel about the size of a small dinner plate. I hoped by the time I pulled on to the main roadway that the defroster would be in high gear and hot enough to clear my windshield. I made it to the minor accident alright, I don't know how. These were the kind of nights that added up to me wanting to go to greener pastures as far as a larger department in a warm climate.

THE CITY IS CALLING

t was snowing really bad, and I got a stolen car report call. I ended up in an old farmhouse in the middle of nowhere. I finished my report and was walking down the steps toward my patrol car when both feet literally slid forward from underneath me, and I went airborne landing on my back on the snow. The steps had been covered with snow and ice to the extent they were sloping. I laid on my back for what seemed like five minutes looking up at the snowing sky, thinking to myself, I have to get out of this place.

After doing standup comedy for my fellow classmates and then performing with a band after high school graduation, people would tell me you should go to Hollywood. One teacher told me that I should follow my dreams of the entertainment business and go to Hollywood. I was always a fan of the L.A. Lakers since the early 1970's when Jerry West was playing. I also was a fan of the Oakland Raiders, and for some unknown reason I already had sights on California, even if I wasn't aware of it.

Like most cops I was inspired by shows like Police Story, Dragnet and Adam 12. I read all the Joseph Wambaugh books. There was a book called Batman and Robin about two wild New York City cops. For some reason, I was infatuated with New York City. I don't know why, I had never been there. We lived 5 hours from New York. Twenty four years old, and I had never been to New York City.

Although things happened from time to time in Livingston County, it was a very rural small Sheriff's Department. I had a divorce, and after almost four years of some really lonely nights, I was becoming depressed. One night in the dead of winter I remember being at a U-turn on Route 390 near Dansville during a snowstorm. Two hours went by and I only saw one vehicle, and that was a snowplow. I don't think that counts. Those freezing winter nights patrolling in the middle of nothing can start to get to you. I started feeding my subconscious mind with a deep desire for going to work at a large metropolitan police agency. I kept that thought constantly on my mind.

The largest Sheriff's Department in the area where one of my good friends worked was the Monroe County Sheriff's Department which encompasses the city of Rochester. They have around 200 deputies. I passed the test, but was never called for an interview or to continue with the process. Next, I took the test for the New York State Troopers. They have about 10 openings for 10,000 applications, and you basically have to score over 95 and they give military credits which can put you over 100. So I knew right away I didn't score well enough. The City somewhere kept calling me.

I saw an ad in a police magazine for the New York City police exam. I made an application and received my entrance card to take the exam at the Norman Thomas High School in Manhattan. So off to New York by train we went: my mom, aunt Ginny and me. We stayed at the Hotel Lexington. How did we ever not go to New York before this? I fell in love with the city right away. All the sights, sounds and lights. This city is alive with energy, and it was infectious. This was 1982. It would be more than 10 years before Giuliani would become Mayor and clean the city up. Grand Central was not grand when we visited. An amazing building filled with derelicts and homeless. They were laying all over Grand Central Station. There must have been hundreds of the homeless laying around, on benches and on the floor. Times Square was a dangerous place you didn't want to be around late at night. It was mostly seedy strip clubs and smut shops. On every corner there were aggressive window washers. Angrily turn one away and you might hear the crack of the squeegee across your windshield.

I loved it, this is what I was looking for. I was losing my mind on those early morning back roads of Livingston County. This is what I wanted. Put me in the worst crime-ridden neighborhood.

My mom and aunt Ginny loved shopping at all the big stores, especially Macy's.

I didn't have a good read as to how I did on the test. Months later, I received a letter in the mail informing me that I was on band three.

Thirty five years later, and my wife and I have been going to New York together since 1998. I'm amazed how safe and wonderful New York is now. I look at Grand Central and think back to my first visit, and the stark contrast between then and now. Grand Central with its cafes and restaurants. Times Square and the theatre district all lit up and full of tourists until all hours of the night. Most of the tourists have no idea what a mess Times Square and Grand Central used to be. The subways were not safe. Today my wife and I have no qualms about riding the New York subways at any hour of the day or night. Manhattan is the easiest city in the world to get around. It's an island; you can only go so far. All the avenues run north and south. All the streets run east and west. If you're going from a higher number street to a lower number, you take a downtown train. If you're going to a higher number, you take an uptown train. By your second visit to Manhattan, you start knowing where the landmarks are and how to get there.

One day I was reading the Police Product News law enforcement magazine, and I saw a full page ad that read, "Ride the strip, we pay the gas." It had a Sheriff's car driving on the Sunset Strip under the Hollywood sign. "Join the Los Angeles County Sheriff's Department, call 1-800- a deputy." Wow, something about just the word Los Angeles. That was Hollywood. That was California. It had been about two years since I first visited my grandmother Anita at her West Palm Beach Florida condo. On that February day we left the Rochester NY airport under gray skies and 17 degrees. I was amazed when less than three hours later we landed in Miami Florida with bright sun and 82 degrees. What the fuck, that did it. I'm leaving that god forsaken upstate New York. I will work where it is summer 12 months of the year. Why would we live for three months of summer and nine months of hibernation waiting for the three months.

I couldn't dial 1-800-a-deputy fast enough. I called L.A.P.D too, and they both sent out applications. L.A.P.D basically told me I could apply, but they were not looking for white males, and I really needed military points because anything less than a 105 was not going to make it. When my Sheriff Dick Kane found out I was applying to the L.A. Sheriff's Department, he was excited and could not have been more encouraging. He told me that he had been out to California for a Sheriff's and Chief of Police conference, and he had met the Sheriff. He said it was the best department in the country, and he would give me time off to go test. He said if I didn't make it, I always had a job with him. So, I had no excuse not to go for it.

There were no obstacles in my way except those I could create myself. That wasn't going to happen. Too many nights on a lonely U-turn in the middle of winter. Now I had hope of future achievement and dreams fulfilled. I sent in my application package, and in short time I received a list of dates that would allow me to fly in to Los Angeles and complete my testing as an out of state applicant. I had an aunt and uncle who lived in Santa Monica, and two friends from high school who were living in Long Beach I could stay with. I stayed with my friends Jim and Karen Goodburlett and stopped in to visit my aunt and uncle while on this trip.

The L.A Sheriff's department had been aggressively recruiting out of state applicants and had a system set up to process them through all phases in four days. First, I took the written test. There were some weird questions, some having to do with flag recognition, and to be honest I guessed on about 20 of the questions. They scored it in a weird way too. I scored something like a 32, and you had to be above 30. I had just passed, and so on the same day we were shuffled off to take the physical agility test. This test involved wearing a belt which was weighted to simulate the same weight as a gun belt you would wear in the field. First you scale a six foot wall, walk on a narrow balance beam, run about fifty yards, climb through a window opening and then climb a 12 foot chain link fence. Next, you run the remaining length of a lap around the track before operating an arrest simulator and dragging a 150lb dummy twenty feet. You had to do this in less than 2 minutes and 50 seconds. I completed it in 2 minutes and 47 seconds. The good lord was with me on that day for sure. That was it for that day of testing.

The next day we were scheduled to have our oral interview at the Hall of Justice 211 W. Temple Street, L.A. I remember the oral panel being three or four people, and it was very lowkey. They seemed to give me some respect as a current police officer, and the questioning was not that intense. After my interview, I went to Universal Studios and took the tour. The next day I was given my first phase medical which was a stress, flexibility, eyes, ears and strength test. All my testing, complete I flew back to New York and went back to work. All I could do at this point was wait.

A few months later, I received a call from my background investigator who told me my case had been assigned to him. He told me that I passed everything so far and would be continuing in the process. He interviewed me over the phone. He told me that out of state applicants have to take a polygraph exam. He said I could fly out to take the polygraph or enter the academy and take it then, but if I didn't pass I would be removed from the academy. I told him I was not going to quit my current job until I had the next one, so I was choosing to fly out to take the polygraph exam.

I flew back to California a month or two later to take my polygraph exam. I was scheduled to take the exam at 1pm. That morning I received a call from my background investigator, asking me if I had any plans for that evening in case the exam went long, and I told him no.

I arrived at my appointment time and was directed into the small room to take my polygraph. There was nothing in the room except one chair next to a desk with the machine and chair behind it. All the walls were bare except one small mirror, which I found out later was a two way mirror. After I filled out a one hundred question form, they had me sit in this room alone for about 30 minutes. Later I found out from my background investigator that he and the operator were watching me from behind the two way mirror. All part of the polygraph exam. Finally the operator came in by himself, and my background investigator watched from behind the mirror. The operator asked me to be patient; this was his first test. Then he said he was kidding, and he was actually was one of the top ten examiners in the country. I would later find out the latter was true. He was one of the best in the country.

I passed the exam and had a meeting with my background investigator before going back home. He told me if I got hired I would have to start in the jail as all deputies do prior to being assigned to a patrol station. He was telling me how the L.A. County jail system had over 20,000 inmates, and drugs were trafficked in the jail and murders occurred in the jail. He said it could be very dangerous and that deputies were assaulted on a daily basis. This seemed unreal to me. Our jail in Livingston County had about 30 inmates, and my hometown only had 4,000 people. He told me to go home and wait for notification. He told me that he would be submitting my package and recommending me for hire, but that didn't mean necessarily that I would be chosen for hire.

Before heading back to New York, my friends Jim and Karen took me to Tijuana Mexico. One of their Mexican friends who lived in Long Beach went with us as a guide. He took us to all these back street bars that mostly locals went to. This was my first time being out of the country. We went to one backstreet dive, and behind the bar there was a big jar that had a sign on it: "Try our snake tequila." In the jar was a full size coiled snake soaking in the tequila. It was pretty good, I think.

We were walking back to the U.S. Border near Tijuana and stepped over some cement circular steps in the dirt. About ten Federalies stopped us. Our Mexican friend translated. He told us they claimed we walked over sacred fountains disrespecting the country, and they wanted money or marijuana. I told him I would just show them my police identification, and we would be on our way. He said don't take out your badge, they will just take it. He spoke to them in Spanish and then turned to us and said he told them to take him to jail, that his grandmother who lived on the hill would bail him out in the morning.

They let us go, and I said, "I didn't know you had a grandmother in Mexico."

He said, "I don't, but they might have spoken English, and they were just trying to strong arm us for money. They don't like Mexicans who live on the other side."

Wow, my education was already starting. I was happy to get back to the USA and head back home to New York and await my fate.

BIG DECISION

Everyone at the Department knew that I went out to Los Angeles to test for the Sheriff's Department. I was in my fifth year on the Department, and I was very close to my mom and dad, along with lifelong friends. Detective Jack York, who would go on to be the next Sheriff of Livingston County, met with me to discuss my decision. "You have been here five years and developed a great reputation, are you sure you want to walk away from that?" he asked. He added, "There are victims everywhere who need good police officers to respond to their aid. Wherever you decide to serve, you will be an asset to the department."

I had several of these visits from trusted friends and advisers who were causing me to take pause, which in retrospect was a good thing. My mom and dad were just always supportive of whatever I wanted to do, and they really wanted me to be happy in whatever I did. They never said a discouraging word to any of my endeavors. My mom was born in San Diego and lived in Los Angeles for several years. So when I broached the subject to my Grandma Schnurr, she said, "Oh dear, you will love it in California. It is a great place, and you will have all sorts of adventures." This was my worldly grandma who had lived and traveled all over the world, so her word carried great weight. This was a definite intention on my part. I didn't have all my eggs in one basket. I had applications to many other police agencies (in warm climates, of course). I had submitted applications to Fort Lauderdale, Miami, Dallas, and Houston Police departments. In the early '80s, Houston was booming, and they were aggressively recruiting nationwide. The L.A. Sheriff's Department was on it. I had completed all my testing in L.A. before I even got my written results from the NYPD.

It was December 1, and I was watching TV in my apartment in Caledonia when I got a phone call. The voice said, "This is the L.A. Sheriff's Department. Do you want a job?" In that very moment, I didn't know how I was going to answer. I was caught off guard, and the person on the phone spoke in a stern manner when they asked the question. Out of the blue, I said, "Yes." He asked me how much time I needed. I told him I needed a few weeks to give notice to the Department and get things in order. He gave me the impression they needed me to start right away. "Be at Sheriff's Headquarters 211 West

Temple Street Los Angeles on December 21 at 8 am, " he said. December 21, 1983. Four days before Christmas was my starting date. Later I would find out that my academy class would not start until January 27, 1984. What an asshole. I didn't need to be there December 21. I would find out that a department of almost 10,000 deputies had more than a few assholes.

The big decision had been made. My friends from the Livingston County Sheriff's Department had a big party for me and gave me gifts. I still have a special stein with my years of service on it that I look at from time to time and think of the night that they gave it to me. I had a 1979 Chevy Impala with t-tops, and my plan was to drive to California with a stop in Kansas City Missouri where my cousin Bobby and his wife Joan were living. I packed up the car and said my goodbyes to mom and dad. It was pretty emotional, but I made it. My next stop was in Rochester. I visited my good friend Tom Vasile, his wife and a couple of friends. We had coffee, and then they presented me with a gold key chain that was inscribed "don't forget us." Driving away and seeing my friends in the rearview mirror waving goodbye broke me up. I drove the rest of the day and continued driving through the night. Except for a couple stops to rest my eyes, I drove for 24 hours before checking into a motel.

The next day I arrived in Kansas City Missouri, and the city was all decorated for Christmas. I stayed over one night with my cousin before heading out the next morning. When I got to the Colorado mountains driving through Vail, I ran into trouble. It was a blizzard, and I had to slow to a crawl and have two wheels off the side of the road to maintain enough traction to keep moving. It seemed like I was in the mountains for several hours with zero visibility. I made it through. People asked me why I took that route, and it was because triple-A gave me that route. Numerous people said they should have given me the southern route. They could have gotten me killed going through those Colorado mountains during a snowstorm. I had a lot of open road until I saw the lights of Vegas. It was my first time seeing the lights of Vegas, which were very exciting and impressive. I didn't stop; I kept on driving.

The sight I'll always remember was going over the Kellog Hill on the 10 Freeway westbound and seeing the Los Angeles Skyline for the first time. And this was it. I wasn't coming out to test or visit anyone. I was now living here: Los Angeles, the City of Angels.

SWEARING IN

I pulled up to my aunt and uncle's house at 2111 Pier Avenue in Santa Monica, and this would be my home for about a month. I think it was a Saturday that I arrived. On Monday morning, December 21, 1983, I went to the Sheriff's Headquarters at 211 W. Temple Street in Los Angeles where I would be sworn in as a Deputy Sheriff. They don't do that anymore. We were actually sworn in prior to going to the academy and receiving any training. We got our badge and I.D. I think we even got our service weapon and were told to take it home and put it away until we received weapons training. We were sworn in and received our assignments as "off the streeters." Most of our group were assigned to custody facilities. Some courts and myself and about four others were assigned to the pre-employment division of personnel right there at the Hall of Justice. Wherever you were assigned, everyone knew your status as an "off the streeter" and that you had not graduated from the academy yet. I would work as an off the streeter until I entered the academy on January 27, 1984. Class 221.

THE ACADEMY

In recent years there was a TV show called The Academy which profiled the L.A. Sheriff's Academy. I thought this was great because it's hard to tell someone what it's really like. So if you check out the show, you will have an idea of what academy life is like.

Putting my experience in perspective, I went to a part time academy in upstate NY Comprising about 20 cadets. We had instructional classes and some range instruction. This L.A. Sheriff's Academy was no joke. Drill instructors who were tough and took pride in a high attrition rate. These drill instructors modeled the drill instructors of the Marine Corps in everything they did. There was a big emphasis on physical fitness, especially on running. This was tough on me. I had always put a big emphasis on gaining muscle and size, so I did next to nothing regarding cardio health. Our class started with 130 cadets, and we would all run in formation through the streets of East Los Angeles. That's where the academy was, on Sheriff's Road. I still remember some of the jodies we would sing while running. "18 weeks of living hell, just work the county jail, I won't cry and I won't moan, soon I'll be at Firestone, sound off, 1-2 sound off, 3- 4, bring it on down now, 1-2-3-4."

There was big time emphasis on academics with weekly tests, big time emphasis on physical fitness with weekly tests, big time emphasis on tactics with weekly tests and evaluations on everything. And you couldn't excel in the training and be an asshole to your fellow cadets. You were required to turn in evaluations on the fellow cadets in your platoon. And if you got the attention of the D.I.'s in a negative way, you would find yourself as the next Class Sergeant, and you didn't want that job. At least I didn't. Some cadets with military experience liked it because they already knew the protocol of issuing military commands. I remember Class Sergeants drenched in sweat just trying to dismiss us for the day. The commands were something like, "Class, upon my command we will fall out of this classroom formation on to the grinder south of the solid white line facing north at attention where we will be dismissed for the day." That's not exactly it, but you get the idea, and if one word was out of place or in the wrong order the D.I.'s would be yelling, "No No No! Do it again!" Sometimes it took us 30-45 minutes to get dismissed for the day. It would already be 6 pm, and you had to go home get some food, clean and shine your gear, do your homework assignment and be back at the academy at 5 am. But like the military, sensory overload and sleep deprivation was a tool to create stress and cause the weak of mind and body to reveal themselves, so they could be washed out before they would be in a position to get themselves or someone else killed in the real world. The drill instructors were constantly checking cars and lockers, and if they found a car or locker unlocked, someone or a group would be on security detail and writing research papers for days.

Right there at the academy they had "Laser Village." it was like a small little town square to do training. There was a mockup of a bank, a store and a two story residence. We were constantly being trained and evaluated on handling mock scenarios and building entries. There was a trailer that would put you through shoot and don't shoot scenarios on a video screen. It would show where your shots would hit or not hit the suspect. Then there was the actual shooting range at the Wayside Honor Rancho, a jail compound at the north end of the county. This range was amazing. There were numerous outdoor shooting ranges for handgun, shotgun and long rifles. They had a Hogan's Alley where you walk along between mock buildings, and a wooden cutout of a suspect would pop up—ladies carrying babies would spring up from another direction. It was just like the movie Dirty Harry with Clint Eastwood. This was the real deal; I was not in Livingston County anymore. They had a range for Skeet and Trap shooting.

Then there's the gas house. Our class would line up to go through this small building with two or three small rooms in it. There was some type of smog pumped into the building to make the visibility near zero. And we would have to enter one end of the building and find our way out the other side. The entire time they were pumping tear gas in the building. As you made your way in the line, you saw your fellow cadets exiting the building, falling to their knees and gasping for air. Some were vomiting as instructors sprayed their faces with a hose. This was great training because in a real life situation where tear gas or pepper spray is deployed, half the time you're going to get a good dose yourself. It feels like your skin is burning and you're not going to be able to breath, but you know your skin isn't burning and you are going to regain full breath. It lessens the likelihood of panic when you already have experience being exposed.

I think we had a week or maybe two at the range. Most everyone loved the range training. Some may have liked it more for the relaxed atmosphere than the weapon training. Because of the inherent dangers involved with so many cadets shooting live rounds, every effort was made to make it a non-stress environment. The range staff had a priority on safety and instruction with the intent on everyone being safe and gaining skill in their shooting abilities with all types of weapons. So there wasn't the yelling and screaming as in a normal day at the academy. They really did want everyone to gain proficiency in their shooting and pass the range qualification. Not being able to qualify with your duty weapon meant being disqualified from the academy. Even those that initially failed were allowed to remediate with some one on one training. These range masters were the best of the best and very good teachers. Not very many cadets were washed out of the academy because of not being able to qualify with their weapon.

Another phase in our academy training that was amazing was the driver's training. The driver's training division is located at the Pomona Fair Grounds. They teach vehicle and motorcycle driving skills not only to cadets of the department but also to other agencies. They have a pursuit course and it is stressful and fun, just like a real pursuit. You get to chase an instructor while a speaker inside the car is blaring a siren and you are broadcasting over the radio. The instructor sitting in the front with you is on your side. They coach you as to how to take the apex of the turns and emphasize when you should be on the breaks and when you should be on the accelerator. You put a lot of stress on yourself because everyone in the class is watching you, and you are being evaluated by the instructors. In Livingston County I had driven in more than ten high speed chases and I was not the best during the academy training, but it was great fun and I had no problem passing.

They had another driving scenario where you drive straight down a center lane and in front of you are three streetlights, each with their own lane. One straight ahead in your lane and one to the right and left of you. All three lights stay red until just before you get to them, and then one turns greens. While you maintain your speed, you have to steer into the green lane without hitting the cones that are separating the lanes. You run through this five or six times. If the light turns green in the center lane, all you do is continue driving straight. You have to fight the urge to try and anticipate which lane is going to turn green. I thought the hardest part of the course to pass was the driving in reverse portion. You have to negotiate this serpentine course of cones driving in reverse at what seems like too fast a speed. It's probably only 20 miles per hour, but going in reverse negotiating cones puts the stress on. Passing the driver's training is mandatory, and you will be allowed to remediate like the range. But also like the range qualification, if you can't pass the driver's training portion of the academy, you will wash out.

For our final role playing exams, which are a must pass, we went to Warner Brothers movie studios in Burbank. They brought in role players who dressed the parts of gang members and other criminal types. Volunteers posed as people involved in a domestic violence situation. There were several scenarios that you and your partner would have to handle. Right before the exercise, the instructors gave you the scenario that you were about to handle. They might have told you, for example, that you were answering a call of a domestic violence. The dispatcher told you that the husband threatened the wife with a gun. Then you were evaluated on how you handled the call, starting with how you approached the building and your interaction with the participants, victims and suspects. You were evaluated on your officer safety tactics. In some scenarios the role players were instructed to be somewhat uncooperative if you didn't take control of the situation as you should. This was one of the final big tests before graduation. Everything kind of leads up to this day.

It was a long tradition of the Sheriff's Academy to be held in East L.A. on Sheriff's Road. In May of 1984, the academy moved from East LA. to Whittier. Our class was to be the last to start at East L.A. and the second to graduate from the new Whittier Academy. A select group of cadets were chosen to run carrying the flag from the old academy to the new location, a distance of about 15 miles. As of this writing, the Academy is moving back to East Los Angeles.

* * *

My first couple months were tough for me at the academy. Most cadets had a support team of family and/or spouse to help them out with meals, studying, and preparation of equipment. Just prior to starting the academy, my aunt and uncle said they were glad to help me get started and allow me to stay on their couch for a couple weeks, but it was time for me to get an apartment of my own, and they were right. My first apartment was on Berryman Avenue in Culver City. Culver City is best known as the home of Metro-Goldwyn-Mayer Studios. It's also still home to Sony Pictures Entertainment. My apartment was about 3 miles from the beach and Marina Del Rey. I loved the location. One of the reasons I wanted to come to Los Angeles was to be near the ocean.

After moving in, I met with the apartment manager in his office. He was man in his late 70's. I'll never forget our conversation that day. I told him my story, and my history of working for the Livingston County Sheriff's Department out of Geneseo NY I asked him if he knew where that was. He turned to a picture on the wall behind him. It was an aerial view of a lake with no cottages on it. He told me that was a picture of Conesus Lake before there was one cottage on it. I'm not sure, but it had to be taken in the 30's or 40's He told me at the time, but I can't remember now. He had once lived near the lake. Come on, that's serendipity. What's the chance of that? So this would be my home during my academy times. A one bedroom apartment with a mattress on the floor and a kitchen table with four chairs.

I found out that famed Golds Gym was about a five minute drive from my apartment in Venice. Rumor had it that all you had to do was show your L.A. Sheriff's badge and you got a membership for free. I showed up at the counter and met the owner and professional bodybuilder Pete Grymkowski. Wow, this was amazing! Pete Grymkowski: winner of Junior Mr. USA, Junior Mr. America, Mr. America, Mr. World. He and two other partners had bought Golds Gym in 1979. Pete Grymkowski was from Rochester NY, and here I was talking to him. He gave me my membership right on the spot.

I had been reading bodybuilding magazines since I was 15 and started lifting weights. I poured over every magazine to learn all I could to assist me in gaining weight and size. I traveled to Harrisburg,

Pennsylvania to see a professional bodybuilding competition. And now here I was at the mecca of bodybuilding. I was trying to work out and not be too star struck by who was working out in the same gym that I was in. Lou Ferrigno, before the Hulk. Actor Carl Weathers. It was an amazing time. I felt I was living the dream.

Class 221 started the academy journey in January of 1984 and graduated in May of that same year. It was a ceremony filled with speeches and gathering of family for pictures. I was so proud to have Mom and Dad fly from New York to be present for and celebrate my graduation. My Aunt and Uncle were there too. We had a great time. My mom and dad found the house on Glendower Avenue where my mom had lived as a very young girl. They rang the buzzer, and the owner let them in to see the house. He was some music producer. I don't remember his name now, but that was really something.

JAIL ASSIGNMENT

My first assignment was Men's Central Jail in downtown Los Angeles. Ah, the worst of the worst; just where I wanted to be! This place—a dungeon, to say the least—housed over 6,000 inmates. The hardcore awaiting trial, the hardcore that had not been processed yet and were sent to other facilities. The hardcore who had been sent from state and federal prisons for more trials or to testify in someone else's trial as a character witness, but actually moved down from prison to do a hit. This was a county jail where serial killers could be housed here for years as they awaited trial. They ran drugs, produced their own alcohol and carried out gang hits in this jail. Pretty amazing place.

Your first few weeks in this place as a trainee were high stress, to say the least. After a few weeks, a group of us were told we would be sent to the Wayside Honor Rancho because a new jail was opening there. I was pissed off. I didn't want to be sent to a lightweight place, I wanted to stay here at the dungeon. When our training officers found out we would be transferring to the north jail, they gave it to us hard. As if it could be any harder as far as I was concerned. I was already working on the side of Central Jail they considered the easy side.

My training officer had called me out for a donning of the fire pack drill about five times one day. Later in the day, this giant of a deputy called me into the control booth of the floor. It was just me and him. He had won powerlifting competitions and had been a police officer from another state. He said to me, "Yates, you were a cop for five years. Your training officer is a pussy. Next time he gives you any shit, tell him to fuck off. You don't have to take his bullshit."

I thanked him but decided to stay on the humble path, at least while I was on training. This deputy who had the talk with me was a badass. Because of his size, some large inmates had expressed an interest in taking him on one on one. Legend has it he did, and kicked their ass without much reporting. I didn't see any of that firsthand. So in a few weeks, about 30 of us were off to our new jail assignments at the Wayside Honor Rancho in Valencia, California, about 30 miles north of downtown L.A.

* * *

This jail facility was amazing; it was a small town itself. The shooting range was located on the property and a working farm. They had a dairy farm where the inmates worked taking care of and milking the cows. There was a pig farm where the inmates worked, and an equestrian center. There were acres of fields with all sorts of crops. When I arrived in 1984, they had three jail facilities: minimum, medium and max. Armed deputies worked the main gate controlling all traffic coming and leaving the facility. They had their own laundry facility. I was assigned to minimum security compound. This turned out to be the best assignment. It was comprised of barracks like you saw in the show Hogan's Heroes. There was a row of 8 barracks on one side of the compound, and a row of 8 barracks on the other side of the compound, and in between was a green space with a road in front of each row of barracks. The center sidewalk led from the main office to the mess hall at the center of the compound. There was an upper compound that had five more barracks. Each barracks held about 120 inmates. At any given time the count was around 2,000 inmates. This was an open compound and it was just like a little town. There was a baseball field, chapel, woodshop and mess hall. All open barracks, no cells.

Each inmate had a green jumpsuit and in the front left breast pocket they had to have their yellow barracks card which had the barracks number they were assigned to stamped in black. So deputies would go into the barracks and check to make sure only those assigned were inside. Inmates would roam to other barracks to steal during the day when the inmates were out at work assignments. The inmates would be out working the field jobs, dairy farm, pig farm, equestrian center, range, and would return in the afternoon. As the inmates would return, they would all be searched most of the time. They would either be searched by the deputies assigned to the field crews or by the compound deputies depending on the size of the work detail. Some of the fields bordered the 5 freeway, and drugs would be dropped off in the fields to be picked up by the inmates out on the work details to be brought back to the compound to be used or sold.

We would actually make drug arrests in the compound for heroin, cocaine and marijuana. For minor violations, like being in the wrong barracks, they would get a ticket. The violation would be marked on the back of their card, and the ticket turned in to the office. At a later time after the count time, the inmates would be called down to the Sergeant's Court. A sergeant would sit at a desk in the office acting as a judge. The inmates would be called up to the desk, the charge would be read to the inmate, and he could give his side of the story. Usually the inmates were given extra duty either in the kitchen or some other clean-up crew.

For serious violations or repeat offenders, the inmates could be assigned to what was called the nickel crew. Group 5 was basically a chain gang. The inmates would be walked to a location to perform some hard labor or to clean up along the freeway by the jail property. Sometimes they actually would be marched out to a field where they would break rocks. The only difference from the old type chain gangs you saw in the movies was that the inmates weren't chained. This was the early 80's, a different time. It wasn't too many years later because of the optics and changing times, Group 5 discipline crew was discontinued.

Some of the jobs at the ranch as it was called were filled by Correction officers. A classification of county employee that had been discontinued, but in the early 80's there were many still working. They wore uniforms that looked like jail deputy uniforms, but the patches said "Correction Officer" instead of "Deputy Sheriff." New deputies assigned to the different work crews would work with a corrections officer who had worked in these positions for many years. The deputies would work their mandatory jail assignments until they went to patrol. If an inmate in the compound committed a serious crime which might include using or selling drugs, assault with a deadly weapon, or battery on a peace officer, they would be handcuffed and basically arrested as if they were on the street. They would be taken in the back of the police car to the maximum (max) jail located a few hundred yards up from the minimum compound. This was a hard celled jail similar to Men's Central Jail in downtown but on a smaller scale. The deputy would write the police report and the inmate would be charged with the additional crime. A jail detective would file the charge or charges with the court.

So originally I was pissed off for being transferred from the Central Jail out to the ranch, but it turned out to be a great thing. Going from a lock down dungeon with stink and no windows to this open compound, fresh air and sunshine. If you have to work in the jail, this was ideal. I was working a foot beat similar to a small town. We made drug arrests, assault arrests, all sorts of arrests. We became proficient in the same forms we would be using when we got out to patrol. I actually felt like a real cop working the minimum compound assignment.

Twice a day, there was a count time. Once in the morning and once in the evening when all inmates had returned from the field jobs. All the inmates would line up in rows in front of their barracks while the deputies called in the count to the office over their radios. Many times the count would not match what was currently recorded at the office. The inmates could be standing out in the sun in this formation for an hour. Usually an inmate that wasn't on the current count would be located. They might have been transported to the max jail, taken downtown, or still at their work assignment. The inmates and deputes would be out in this formation until the count was cleared. A deputy would broadcast from the main office and you would hear over the speakers in the compound, "Count is clear, count is clear." this would signal to the inmates that they could return to their barracks or otherwise head to Sergeant's Court or extra duty jobs.

Every once in a while there would be an actual escape. They could get out during the night by cutting through the fence or not return while they were out working a field assignment. Most of the inmates assigned to the minimum compound were in on lightweight misdemeanor charges and didn't have much time left to do. So the incentive to escape and risk being charged with escape which would get you another year locked in a hard cell was too high. Like the deputies, inmates realized they were in the best place they could be if you had to be in jail, so even they didn't want to mess that up. But escapes would happen, and the compound would be locked down and a big search would begin. Hound dogs would respond, a helicopter would fly overhead and many times the escaped inmate would be found in one of the fields or on a road nearby.

We had our little town within a town: the minimum compound

and the other two jails, medium which was also an open compound with barracks, and maximum hard celled jail. The Wayside Honor Rancho had a police car that patrolled the entire property. The position was filled by jail personnel that had previous patrol training. There was another vehicle that was filled with jail deputies used to transport prisoners between jail facilities at the ranch and also to other jails in the county.

During visiting the correction officers operated buses bringing the visitors from the parking lot at the main gate up to the jail facility where the visiting center was, a distance of about two miles. Deputies were assigned on foot and patrol cars to monitor people coming on to the jail facility to visit inmates. Even though there were warning signs everywhere, four to five people every weekend would be arrested and taken to jail for bringing drugs and/or weapons on to a jail facility, which was a Felony. They would be booked at the nearby Santa Clarita Sheriff's Station. People would actually drive on to the jail property to visit an inmate and be arrested for Driving Under the Influence.

The minimum compound was a very safe and enjoyable assignment. But it could turn dangerous very quickly. With 2,000 inmates, many of which were active gang members, we had to constantly monitor tension in the compound. Several riots have broken out at the facility over the years. There could be some real hardcore gang members who just happened to be doing time on a misdemeanor charge. Although classification was supposed to weed those individuals out and not assign them to the minimum facility, it would happen. Every so often there would be a hit at the minimum compound or just a shanking over who knows what that would lead to a death. We were always searching for and finding homemade weapons. The inmates had access to all sorts of materials to make weapons from. They were working in the kitchen, laundry, woodshop, dairy and pig farms. They made great shanks out of metal pieces removed from the steel bunk beds. They could take apart the security razors to get the blade and then melt the end of a toothbrush and sink the blade in the toothbrush before the plastic hardened, which made a great slicing tool.

We had use of metal flashlights and saps, but all too often we would resort to using our fists to protect ourselves, which was very stupid. I learned firsthand how stupid that was. I had a training officer in the jail who had been a boxer, and he would hit the heavy bag in the gym consistently. When he hit someone with his fist, he knew what he was doing. Not only did he know how to hit, he knew where to hit. I think he broke nine jaws in a row. I thought I could punch like him, and I was wrong. One pm shift during the inmate feeding, I sent an inmate who had been smuggling food out of the mess hall down to the office, with the intention of rolling him up later (sending him to a different facility). He suddenly turned and started running toward me. In protection of myself, I tried to throw a hard left cross to his face. I missed the mark and caught him square on the forehead. He went down like a ton of bricks, and I almost did too. I had broken my hand by hitting his forehead. That was an idiot move that was painful and caused me 6 weeks in a soft cast. Not to mention a light duty assignment at the main office. I don't know which was more painful, the hand or the assignment.

When you were assigned to your mandatory custody assignment, you picked the stations you wanted to go to. The stations you pick and how fast the movement is determines how fast you could get out of the jail. I wanted no part of the jail. I came out to this big agency to work the streets in the most crime infested areas. Depending on attrition and a bunch of other factors, the rotation from custody to patrol varied. Some deputies went to patrol in six months and some went after five years. I had picked the fastest stations, but when I entered my second year in custody, I was becoming disgruntled and downright pissed off.

I was ready to quit and go to another department. I applied again to L.A.P.D and I got a notice that the N.Y.P.D was getting to band three from the last test. The band three I was still on, I just needed to contact them and arrange for out of state testing to get my name back in play. Perfect timing; I was in. Everyone told me to hang on and that it would be worth the wait. They told me story after story of deputies who left the department only to return. I wasn't hearing any of that. I made arrangements to fly to New York to get back in the process. So in August of 1986, I flew back to New York.

I arrived at Newark Airport in the morning, and something was going on in the city because I couldn't get a hotel room for less than $500. I slept in the airport until it was time to leave for my appointment at the NYPD Academy. At the academy I met with a guy who had been on the job for over 20 years in every assignment there was. He was a great guy who spent many years on the streets. He said, "NY is the asshole of the Earth, don't do this. I will test you if that's what you want, but I'm telling you, stay in California. You're living the dream, look how much money your making. It's up to you, but my advice is to stay in California."

I wasn't be able to be tested until the next day, and I still couldn't find a hotel room in Manhattan for under $500. I'm sure I could have, but I was not on my game. I think I was over tired from sleeping in the Newark Airport. I made a decision that day to return to L.A. and continue with the L.A. Sheriff's Department. As I look back on it, maybe that decision saved my life. There is no doubt I would have chosen to live and work in Manhattan. So when 9/11 happened, I'm sure I would have responded in some way or another. I either would have gotten killed on the day of the attack, or as many of the those that responded are doing now, died of cancer years later from the smoke inhalation.

After returning to L.A. I had to keep buys while in the jail so I wouldn't go crazy waiting for my patrol assignment. I signed up for a comedy writing class in the San Fernando Valley. My experience doing stand-up for my high school classes and after graduation with a local band involved me memorizing other comedians' routines and performing them. I didn't know that wasn't something you were not supposed to do. I didn't know anything about writing my own material. From day one of my comedy writing class, I have only performed my own written material. Comedians often use the same premises to write material, so sometimes you will hear similar material. It's not stolen but based on the same premise. You will have similar set ups and punch lines. I have even thrown out material I have written because later I saw someone do something similar, and I never wanted that reputation of stealing someone else's joke.

I can't remember the name of the guy who taught the class. He was a great guy, and near the end of our class he had a good friend of his who was a working comedian come talk to us. His name was Ray Combs. Wow, this guy was inspiring. This was 1986, and at the time he was getting paid great money to be the warmup act for numerous TV shows. He talked about coming to L.A from Ohio to make it in stand-up. He had to work odd jobs by day and perform at open mics at night. He slept in his car until he could make enough money to have his family join him in L.A. Ray Combs was so inspiring. He was very energetic and upbeat. He stayed after our class to talk with us. There was only about 10 of us in the class, so we had some great personal conversations with Ray.

Our final class was at the L.A. Cabaret which was a comedy club on Ventura Blvd between White Oak and Balboa. Everyone in the class did a 10 minute set, and Ray Combs came and closed the show. He was fantastic, and he killed it of course. Ray Combs said he liked my set and told me I should continue in my comedy pursuits.

In 1987 he landed a great supporting role in the movie Overboard with Goldie Hawn and Kurt Russell. One year later in 1998, he was picked as the new Host of Family Feud. He held that job until he was fired in 1994 to make room for the return of Richard Dawson. The firing was the start of a downhill spiral for Ray. He was in a serious car accident in 1995, leaving him partially paralyzed for a time. He regained his ability to walk but was in constant pain. He got divorced and was hospitalized after trying to kill himself with prescription medication. In 1996 Ray Combs was found dead in his Glendale, Ca home. He had hanged himself. It's hard to grasp how this man I met in 1986 who was so vivacious and talented with a great career would be dead 10 years later at the age of 40.

During this time in the jail I found another obsession to distract me and keep me busy while awaiting to go to patrol. I saw a late night infomercial from Bobby Singer, a blackjack card counter. He was selling a program for the Bobby Singer Method. This was fantastic. I had been to Vegas once since coming to California and fell in love with it. For a career insomniac night person like me, a city with no clocks that never stops is for me. I bought that program by Bobby Singer and devoured it. I read it over many times and began following the plan.

And I bought four or five books on card counting. I not only got proficient, you could probably say I became a semiprofessional card counter. To the point that it became financially profitable for me to fly into Vegas in the morning, card count through the day and then fly home in the evening. I did this five or ten times. Blackjack is the only game in Vegas where what's been played tells you what's left to be played.

The system I used was called a plus minus system. Contrary to what some people believe, card counters keep track of groups of cards, not every card. In this system 7, 8, 9 cards are given the value of zero and are considered neutral cards. The 10's and face cards are given the value minus one, and 2-6 are given the value of plus one. Then you train your eye to keep a running count, looking at two cards. So a 2 card and a king would give you a running count of zero. The two being a plus one and the king being a minus one. You train yourself to look at two cards and see the count of the two cards. So if the next two cards were two sevens, your count would still be zero. The first two cards cancelled each other, the plus one and the minus one. The next two cards, the sevens are zero cards, so you're still at zero.

To increase your proficiency in this skill, you take a deck of cards and remove a card without looking at it. Then you thumb through the deck two cards at a time, and when you get to the end, depending on the number you're at in your count, you will know the value of the card you removed if you counted correctly. Every deck has to count to zero, so if you end with a count of minus one, you know the card you removed has to be a 2, 3, 4, 5 or 6 because you need a plus one count for the deck to be at zero. If you end with zero, you know it is a 7, 8, 9 card. And you keep doing this until you can fan through a deck in less than thirty seconds with a correct count.

I bought my own blackjack table, and I would practice counting seven hands being dealt at a time. I would not only count but do the basic strategy of each hand. The basic strategy just says that in every deal there is a best decision mathematically. So I had flashcards with the basic strategy. If I am dealt an ace and 7, then mathematically I should double if the dealer has a 3, 4, 5, 6 and stand if the dealer has a 2, 7, 8. Otherwise, I should hit. So, I had flashcards with every different combination I could be dealt and on the reverse side of the card what the proper decision would be. I got to know those decisions reflexively, so I wouldn't have to think about it during the deal, and I could concentrate on my card counting.

That was a weird time in Las Vegas. 1985 and 1986. On the one corner was just the Tropicana, and across the street was the Marina. There was no New York, New York, no MGM Grand. The Marina was later bulldozed and replaced with today's MGM. Originally the MGM was where the current Bally's is now. They were knocking down the Sands and soon after that the Stardust. I could actually write a book on card counting, maybe I will. When I was counting this was the time that a group of MIT students were taking Vegas for big bucks with card counting teams. This kept me busy waiting for patrol. And then finally in June of 1987.

LYNWOOD STATION

Finally in June of 1987, I was transferred to patrol. This was exciting. Before going to your unit of assignment after being transferred to the field operations division, you had to attend and pass patrol school. For most deputies a lot of time has passed since graduating from the academy where you learned everything about police work from a field deputy's perspective. And then you go to the jail, which for most deputies is several years. If you're smart, as your time comes near to going to patrol you start preparing yourself. You make sure all your gear and equipment are up to par, and you go on some uniformed ride alongs. Patrol training is very tough and not everyone makes it. Some have to remediate and come back again before passing. And some never make it. One thing that will make it tougher is telling your training officer you did nothing to prepare yourself for patrol while in custody.

When you got to patrol school, there were a couple deputies from your station of assignment who gave you a little orientation. They told you what to expect and what you needed to have before you got to the station. The department had a lot invested in you since the day you applied. When you got to patrol, everyone wanted you to succeed. If you failed field training, the reason or reasons in most cases could be attributed to officer safety. If you don't have good tactics, officer safety is an issue. Unable to remain calm and take control in emergency situations, officer safety is an issue.

I remember Deputy Dave Gutierrez being one of our orientation deputies who came from Lynwood station to monitor those of us who were newly assigned to the station. Not only was it his job to advise us so we would be prepared when we arrived, he also reported back to the station as to what kind trainees were coming. Any problem child could be identified while they were at patrol school. Deputy Gutierrez told us the station was extremely busy. He said some nights there might be so many shooting calls that you wouldn't be able to respond to all of them. This didn't seem possible to me. Sounded like he was telling fairy tales. Remember my perspective, I came from Livingston County in upstate NY sitting in my patrol car on route 390 at a U-turn in the middle of winter and hadn't seen a car in two hours. Now I'm going to a patrol station in south central L.A. where it's so busy and there are so many shootings, you can't even respond to all of them. This is what I wanted. I was a happy person.

I made it through patrol school no problem. Next stop Lynwood Station, 11330 Bullis Road in the City of Lynwood, Ca. Lynwood Station had patrol responsibilities for the unincorporated area of Los Angeles that bordered Watts, Compton and Southgate. Lynwood was also a contract city. The city contracted with the Sheriff's Department to be their police department. At one time they had their own police department. I don't remember why the city dissolved their police force and contracted with the department. It was several years prior to me becoming a deputy. On any given shift, deputies would be assigned to the City of Lynwood, Willowbrook, (county area of L.A.) or East Compton (county area bordering the City of Compton).

To say that the station area was gang infested would not do justice to the amount of gang activity. Here is a list of some of the gangs we had to deal with: 7th street Watts Crips, Carver Park Compton Crips, Mona Park Compton Crips, Neighborhood Watts Crips, Grape Street Watts Crips, Palm and Oak Gangster Crips, Bounty Hunter Bloods, West Side Piru Bloods, 135 Piru gang, Cross Atlantic Piru Bloods, Tree Top Piru Bloods, Lime Hood Piru Blood Gang. Leuders Park Piru Blood Gang, Fruit Town Piru Blood Gang. I won't even list the more than 18 Hispanic gangs in Lynwood's area.

The Crips are signified by wearing the color blue. The Bloods by wearing the color red. Every gang in Lynwood has a territory of control. Every gang member knows the map, where they should and shouldn't go. If you fly (wear) the wrong colors in the wrong place, it's a green light for the gang that controls that area to kill you. So if a Blood gang member gets shot and killed, within hours a retaliatory shooting will occur, and on and on it goes. When a gang war starts over drugs, territory or retaliation, it could go on for quite some time. There was always a string of dead bodies left behind in the wake of every gang war. The first thing I learned was that deputy Gutierrez was not telling fairy tales. This place was jumping off.

* * *

As a trainee you were expected to arrive at least an hour before shift to read the briefing boards and get yourself and your equipment ready for the shift. So by the time your training officer arrived, everything was prepped and ready to go. Part of this process established good habits that would carry you through your patrol career.

One of the most important things was prepping the car for the shift. After you found out what car you were assigned, you had to determine if it was available or still out on the previous shift. Once you had your assigned car, then you would do a physical inspection of the exterior. You had a vehicle inspection sheet which had a picture of the car on it at various angles so you could note any damage to the car. This comes into play when damage is noticed, and then whoever is investigating the damage will backtrack through the vehicle inspection sheets, and the last person who didn't note the damage will be on the hook for claiming responsibility. The watch sergeant is responsible for collecting all the vehicle inspection sheets for the shift. Years later these paper sheets would be replaced by computer entries at the beginning of your shift. Sergeants had to be on their toes with the paperwork. If a sergeant wasn't collecting these inspection sheets, hypothetically you could hold on to your inspection sheet, and if you had any damage or dents during your shift, you could note it on your sheet and slip it in at the end of your shift. I'm sure this never happened.

After you inspect your patrol car's exterior, you have to search the inside of the car, specifically the backseat. When someone is arrested, they should be thoroughly searched prior to being put in the backseat of the radio car. Sometimes this isn't done, or it isn't done thoroughly. Prisoners once in the backseat are able to dump any contraband. Even while handcuffed behind their back, prisoners were able to get rid of all sorts of contraband, weapons and drugs. When we had regular backseats, you would pull the backseat out. When you pulled the seat out, more often than you would think you would find drugs, knives, and even guns under the seat. You should never find anything under the seat. If you do your job right, you search your car prior to starting your shift, and you search it after each arrest and at the end of your shift. If you bring a prisoner in and you find drugs under the seat, you can charge your prisoner with possessing the drugs or other contraband and get a conviction because you can testify that you searched your car prior to your shift and at the end of your shift. And if you're the oncoming shift and find the contraband and you can't link it to a prisoner, you have to write a Found Narcotics Report.

Things will happen, especially at a fast station, where you will be running to your car and responding to an emergency without the chance to do your normal vehicle check. Later these cloth seats would be replaced with hard plastic seats that are bolted right to the car frame. It was impossible to hide contraband anywhere. You might find it on the seat or the floor, but there was no way to push anything under the seat.

After you clear your backseat, depending on the deputies who had the car before, you may have some major cleaning to do. When I first started in patrol, chewing tobacco was a big thing. You might have spit marks down the outside of the doors. There might be spit cups left inside the car. Some deputies would just leave their car a pig sty. You would find all their food remnants. From paper bags, cups, and actual food strewn all over the car.

Next you had to check your Ithaca 12 gauge shotgun. You took that out of the rack and rotated the locking nut which allowed you to twist the barrel and remove it from the gun frame. There you would look down the barrel to make sure nothing was stuffed in there like papers or who knows what. Then you would slide the pump handle forward and pull the trigger as you held a finger over the hole where the firing pin would emerge. If it was firing properly, you would feel the firing pin as it jutted out upon pulling the trigger. Then you would reassemble your shotgun, load it with fresh rounds and replace it in the rack.

I was trained to always have clean windows before we went 10-8 in the field. For the rest of my career I always searched my car, checked my shotgun and cleaned my windows. I would even carry my own window cleaner to make sure I could start my shift with clean windows.

Field training lasted six months. Usually you were with your T/O (training officer) for four months, and on the fifth month you would work in a car by yourself with your T/O as your sister car monitoring your calls and there to back you up or assist you with calls you had trouble resolving. And on the final sixth month you would be back together for final tests and evaluations. This was a perfect world scenario, but with injuries, staffing shortages or some other reason, it might not go as planned. At some time or another your T/O would be assigned training, or have time adjusted for a court case, and then you would ride with another T/O. This could be good or bad. Your temporary T/O might tell you it's a no stress day, and you would have a pretty enjoyable shift. It would depend on a number of factors. Where you were in your training and how you were progressing. All the training officers knew how each of their trainees were doing. So if a trainee was having trouble, when it came time with another T/O, it might get even harder. The T/O you're with might not like your T/O. It was always stressful working with a different one. But everyone works different, so it was good to have exposure to different styles of policing and report writing.

My training officer was Deputy Marvin Washington. I think as of this writing he is still working as either a Chief or Commander. To me, he was the best of the best. He was so smart and just a great trainer. All that and he was a super cop. We had a couple months of very serious training, and as time went on we had more and more times we laughed our asses off together. Lynwood had everything as far as crime was concerned. You got hands-on training for every type of scenario you could think of. Some stations didn't have that available to them, so they had practice scenarios. Not Lynwood, no practice anything. Every day we would work on something different.

I'll call my T/O Marv. Since I'm off training now and we are great friends, I can call him that. One day Marv said, "Today is Heroin Day." He took me to some back alleys where all the hypes hung out. He just called them over to us. He told them they were not going to jail but to show us where they last shot up. These hypes would tell us how long they had been using, where they liked to shoot. They showed us their old tracks, their new tracks. He would show me all the symptoms of someone under the influence of an opiate. We had a pupilometer card on us we could hold up to someone's eyes to measure how small or large a person's pupils were. In the case of opiates like heroin, a person would have pinpoint pupils. In the case of a stimulant, they would be dilated in spite of being in bright sunlight.

After we examined the third or fourth hype. we arrested one for being under the influence of heroin. After visually checking his pockets, Marv had the suspect pull out his pockets. A lot of these hypes were HIV positive. Marv told me deputies would ask these hypes if they had any needles on them before they reach in their pockets. Numerous deputies were stuck with needles reaching into the pockets of a hype who said, "No, I don't have any needles." Then the deputies would have to be tested. We finished booking our hype, and Marv showed me the procedure for noting the track marks and recent punctures where the hype shot up. Then he told me that was the last hype arrest we would be making unless we had to. He didn't like arresting hypes. They had a lot of health issues that could be contagious along with the danger of HIV being transmitted to you by being stuck with a needle. He said when I was off training I could arrest as many hypes as I wanted. Sometimes you had no choice because we would catch them in the act of burglary or other felony they were committing to feed their heroin habit. I continued Marv's policy for avoiding hypes for the rest of my career.

Marv loved getting crooks in stolen cars, and so did I. Maybe I got that from my dad who loved stolen cars too. He was the master back in NY So, I made that my mission. There was a lot of stolen cars rolling around. Gang members loved to steal cars to do their drive by shootings in and whatever crime they were doing. And there were a lot of gang members, so do the math.

Stolen cars are fun to stop, chase and recover. When I started in Lynwood we had no in car computers, so you really had to use your police skills in getting them. There were some obvious tell-tale signs. When you drove in traffic, you were looking inside the cars, and if you saw a rag or a towel draped over the steering column combined with a look at the occupants, good chance it was a stolen car. Sometimes you would look inside a car as you drove through traffic and see a screwdriver sticking out of the column where the key used to go. Good bet it's a stolen car. On occasion the car turned out to be a previously stolen vehicle. It was stolen in the past, and since recovered and returned to the owner, they hadn't repaired the damage to the steering column and/or ignition. We ran a check on every Toyota Camry and Honda Accord we saw with youthful drivers. These cars were the most stolen models in south central L.A. in the late 80's. We got a lot of rollin stolens when I was on training.

I have to stop here and explain our radio system, which is a little complex and hard to understand even when you use it every day. It had to deal with simplex and duplex radio systems. In Livingston County the radio system was one where everyone heard everyone else. So when I called to the dispatcher over my police car radio, the dispatcher heard it along with every other car and portable police radio in the county. Now in L.A. County, it's completely different. I'll explain it and try not to go too deep into the weeds.

Each station has a station dispatcher and person answering phones and typing calls into the system. In East Los Angeles we have the main county dispatchers for the entire county. When a call is typed in, it is sent to the main East L.A. dispatch center and then dispatched to the cars. When I started patrol in 1987, we received all our calls over the radio and had to write them down and produce a paper log for the end of the shift documenting all of our calls. We had to document when we got the call, when we responded, how long it took to get there, how long we were at the call and when we cleared the call. Every log had to be tallied, and each minute of your 480 minute eight hour shift had to be accounted for, and if the numbers were off you had to find the error and correct it. Believe me, that was a nightmare. You could be two hours after your shift trying to fix your log and get it approved.

Fast forward a couple years when the computers were put in the cars, and your log and activity was done for you by the computer. And unless you messed up on your button pushing, your log was done at the end of shift and just had to be printed out. And eventually you didn't even have to do that. So with the computer, you pushed a button when you received the call, a button when you went in route, and a button when you went 1097 (arrived) and 1098 (call completed in service) when you were clear.

When you used the radio in L.A. only the desk and East L.A. dispatchers could hear you. Everyone heard the main dispatcher in East L.A. You could not talk to your desk directly unless you switched to a different channel which was used strictly for the desk to car communication. When you and/or other cars were on this desk channel, you all could hear each other. On the main channel you wouldn't know when other cars were talking, except it made a beep beep when the channel was busy. So before you broadcasted over the radio, you first clicked the button. If someone else was talking, it would beep. If not, then you were clear to talk.

If there was an emergency you decided everyone should be hearing, you broadcasted 1033 (requesting emergency clearance) then the main dispatcher would flip a switch and say, "1033 go, you're on the patch." The other cars would hear "1033 go" and stop whatever they were doing, or at least stop trying to use the radio and listen up to what was happening. Then you would get on the radio, and whatever you were saying would be heard by everyone who was on that channel. For example, you might broadcast you were following a 1029 Victor (reported stolen car), give your location and request additional units to conduct a felony traffic stop. While on the patch mode you would also hear all the other cars, and you could communicate with them. In the meantime, while you were conducting this business on the patch, all other units on that channel couldn't conduct any business over the radio. So you had to try and coordinate your business as quick as you could and then have everyone involved in your incident go to a separate channel so the main dispatcher could drop the patch and return the channel to normal operations.

Back in Livingston County we didn't need this type of system. At any given time the total cars we would have patrolling for the whole county, including all the police departments would be less than 20. L.A. County on a pm shift with 20 plus patrol stations might be fielding 400 police cars. That's not including detective bureaus and special units. So, the radio system is quite complex to say the least.

Back to stolen cars. So when you wanted to run a check on a plate, you would broadcast your car number and 1028, 1029 (registration and warrant check). If the dispatcher was ready to put the plate into the system, he or she would broadcast back to you go ahead with your 1028, and then you would broadcast the plate number. If it was stolen, the dispatcher would advise 1029 Victor, and everyone would hear that and wait for you to get on the patch for coordination or maybe you would be in pursuit. Or maybe it was just abandoned unoccupied, and you would advise that too. So if you were good at getting stolen cars, everyone would become aware of that because of the coordinated felony stop or chase which would follow.

Marv taught me so much. A City of Lynwood car requested assistance after responding to a loud music call. There is a distinction between a request for backup and assistance. Backup was routine, and assistance meant bad shit was happening and needed immediate help. No one at the station liked putting out assistance requests, some kind of ego thing I think. So any time we heard a request for assistance, we rolled hard.

We got to the location in a residential neighborhood of the city, and there were people all over the place. It was a Mexican wedding reception. There were about five police cars there. As we got out of our unit, we heard windows break from the house, and people were yelling and screaming. As we were getting out of the police car, Marv said, "Put your helmet on. This is a Mexican wedding. Soon the Budweiser cans will be flying, trust me."

Just then Sergeant House arrived in his patrol car. Sergeant House was a tall, lanky male black sergeant. He had recently been transferred to Lynwood after being promoted to sergeant from the International Liaison Division of the Sheriff's Information Bureau (media relations). He was a very nice, intelligent man who spoke several languages and was a fish out of water at this assignment. Sergeant House was trying to assemble arriving deputies in his calm voice and trying to keep this situation from escalating out of control. Sergeant House tried to arrange deputies in some kind of formation to enter the large crowd of wedding attendees who were still fighting all over the place. Marv told me to take note of the sergeant and the group of deputies who were not wearing helmets as we were and a few other veterans saying, "They have no idea."

Suddenly like an L.A Dodgers foul ball, a full Budweiser beer can came flying high and fast out of the crowd, hitting Sergeant House on the right side of his head. He was staggered and grabbed the right side of his head. His calm voice was gone as he yelled, "Getem!"

Marv said, "I told you" as we ran toward the crowd pr24 (side handle batons) in hand.

My memory of the next few minutes is a blur. Lawsuits that lasted years came out of this incident. I do remember arrests, and people sent to the hospital that night were in the double digits. I think Sergeant House was processing paperwork from that night for months. That night Sergeant House became fully aware he was not at Sheriff's Headquarters anymore. Like many supervisors, he adapted and transferred out of there as soon as possible. It was not an easy place for a supervisor. Since most newly assigned supervisors transferred out as soon as they could, there was too much happening too often for field sergeants to keep up.

I had some overwhelming days while on training at Lynwood. One day we arrested two in a stolen car. We arrested someone for being under the influence of drugs, and he had a gun. We took three burglary reports. And on the way into the station at the end our shift, we arrested two for being in possession of PCP. Finally the shift was over, and I had started none of these reports. I had not booked the evidence let alone started my log. Sometimes you just didn't know where to start. It was not unusual to get off your shift and see trainees writing reports, return sixteen hours later to start your next shift and see the same trainees still writing reports.

Marv and I mostly worked the Willowbrook Car, which was the unincorporated area of L.A. bordering Watts and Imperial Courts housing projects. If we were lucky, there would be two cars assigned to the area. Years later I heard there were three or more cars assigned to the area. Hard to believe while I was on training, many times it was just us in unit 253.

There were the normal gang killings and retaliation, along with the cocaine wars between drug sellers and controlling gangs. PCP was everywhere. It was wild times. One pm shift they gave us a call; 245 (assault with a deadly weapon) just occurred 109th Street between Alameda Street and Mona Blvd, several down, 253 had the handle. Several down, what the fuck. I got on the radio and coordinated the response of assisting units to create a containment and lock down the crime scene and called for an aero unit.

When we arrived there people lying in the street and crowds of people running all over the place. Later Marv laughed and said when we arrived on the scene, he looked at me and my face went pale. I don't know about that, but maybe it did. All sorts of assisting units arrived. This was a large crime scene and containment area. Marv was telling me, "Direct them where to go and what to do." We had the handle and deputies and training officers were waiting for me to give them a task or assignment. I was directing deputies to containment locations and directing them to conduct interviews and to give me a supplemental report. It's a weird dynamic when you're on training. Walking around the station or anywhere, you know your place. You are polite to everyone and have a very subservient attitude, especially to training officers and also to any deputy no longer on training. In and around the station, you're expected to keep quiet, listen and do what your told. In a field situation during an emergency or operation, you're expected to take control delegate where you need people. You have to dance between these two protocols.

We taped off the entire length of 109th Street from Alameda to Mona Blvd. as a crime scene, a distance of a couple hundred yards. We had three gunshot victims laying on the street, still alive. A deputy was standing over a body in a front yard under an air conditioner. He yelled, "Marv, this one is dead!" Now I had one dead shooting victim and three others who were shot and down on the street. The whole street was a crime scene, and we had a containment area of the surrounding blocks. We didn't know who shot who, but we had it locked down.

The helicopter was overhead, ambulances were arriving for the victims who were still alive. I was manning our makeshift command post. You have to coordinate all these resources. Request a tactical frequency for your operation. You have to advise the desk who is where and doing what. They have to know who is available for the calls that are coming in for other crimes. The watch commander needs a call so he or she knows what's going on. The field sergeant arrives and wants to know what we and everyone else is doing. He knows soon the watch commander and maybe Division Commander or Chief will arrive and ask him the same questions, and he better have the answers.

The suspects were last seen running west from the location between houses. I had about eight cars and fifteen deputies on this containment. Some training officer would have their trainee write everything from the verbal reports from other deputies. My smart training officer taught me to be efficient. He told me to tell every deputy that I assigned a task to give me a supplemental report. Then all I have to do is write the initial crime report and collect all the supplementals and turn them in with the initial crime report. The deputies that went to the hospital to check on the medical condition of the wounded and take their statement wrote me a supplemental report on the statements and medical condition. The dog handler and the deputies that went along on the search gave me a supplemental report. The deputies who interviewed witnesses gave me their supps. A gun was recovered at the scene. The deputy who took control of the weapon and booked it into evidence wrote me a supplemental report on that. So although initially these calls can be overwhelming, in the end once the activity is parceled out and everyone writes a supplemental report on what they did, it's not so bad.

CARVER PARK MASSACRE

I was in my last month or two of training. Marv and I were working the pm shift out of Willowbrook. We received a 245 now call (assault with a deadly weapon). Man with a shotgun in Carver Park, numerous gang members involved. We were the first to arrive at the park, and there must have been over one hundred Carver Park Crips who started running everywhere at the sight of the arriving Sheriff's car. We saw two guys running from the park with handguns, and a gang member just two yards from us threw a sawed-off shotgun to the ground and started running. Marv ran and tackled the suspect within 25 yards while I secured the loaded shotgun. We called for assistance as all the gang members ran to the end of Antwerp Street, where they gathered yelling obscenities and threats all the while throwing their gang signs.

The sergeant arrived, and after the troops arrived, we announced an unlawful assembly and ordered the gang to disperse. Marv taught me to put our car radios on loudspeaker mode and then get on the patch to make the dispersal announcement. There were legal requirements in the announcement which had to be made before you could make an arrest. By making the announcement over the regular radio frequency, you could request the tape of the broadcast later to prove in court that you made the announcement. Here's a shocker; they refused to disperse. We rolled hard to the end of the street. There was a lot of resistance. The taser was used, and physical force was required to make a lot of the arrests. Another caper was my handle.

And I was so happy to have the knowledge of delegating and having supplemental reports written. We made 24 arrests for unlawful assembly mixed in with our 245 suspect and the use of force reports. I think Marv and I broke a station record that day, one call 24 arrests. Marv's friend Joey Fennel was working the jail that day. You should have seen his face when we marched in with 24 in custody. I think the station jail only held 50. We dubbed that day the Carver Park Massacre. For the next year or so whenever we made an arrest or otherwise contacted anyone from Carver Park, they were very cooperative and respectful. We were there a lot. They sold a lot of marijuana at the dead-end of Antwerp Street. Customers came from all over to buy marijuana there. The problem is you make an arrest, and by the time you're done booking, someone else has replaced the seller you arrested. The customers keep coming, so believe me the product is around, and there is always somebody ready to step in and continue the selling.

OFF TRAINING

Training is a stressful time at Lynwood. So when you pass training, or get off training as it's called, it is quite a celebration. There is usually a big party for a group of trainees that have recently finished training. And then you work a one-man car for a while. If you're lucky and you so desire, you can then find a partner to work a two-man car with. I should say a two-person car. I had several female partners that I loved working with and trusted with my life. Personally, I liked working alone. I liked calling all the shots, deciding where to drive, who to stop, when to eat. Most deputies liked working with a partner. I had some great partners while at Lynwood, and we had a great time together. All one person cars are contract cars in the city of Lynwood. And the two-person cars were in the county areas. The county areas had less call activity, so you had more time to be on the hunt. Police work is hunting for humans. It's a lot of fun. I liked working alone, but the city cars got hammered with calls.

There was a parking garage on Imperial Highway near the station where we would park to write reports or finish up our logs before heading into the station at the end of our shift. It was a two-story parking garage, and we parked on the top level which had no cars on it after 5 pm or on the weekends. It was a safe place to park because it was elevated, and you couldn't be seen from the street. You couldn't just park anywhere in Lynwood and write reports by yourself. You would get sniped, shot, or have your throat slashed. But this was a great spot. For some reason, I named it the "Hilton." So after about a year if you asked another car to meet you at the Hilton, everyone— even the desk—knew where you were talking about. A safe place, maybe, or maybe not.

One night near the end of the pm shift, I radioed my roommate Bill Costleigh, who was working a traffic car in the city. I told him to meet me at the Hilton, and he said he was just finishing a ticket and he would be right up. I drove to the parking garage top floor and backed into an empty parking space of my choice so I could face the one ramp controlling access to and from the top of the parking garage. I had my choice since the top level was empty of any cars.

I was finishing a report and looked up to see headlights coming up the ramp. I wrongly assumed it was the front headlights from Bill's police car. I looked down, and a second later a car that was not Bill's or a police car was door to door with mine. The lone male occupant was a big red-headed white guy. He was breathing heavy, and as he came to a stop started yelling at me, "You better fucking shoot me now, shoot me, shoot me now!"

As I started to my car in drive as discretely as possible, I said, "Do you have a gun?"

He said, "I got a fucking 45 right here under my arm."

He had just finished that last part when I jumped on the accelerator. The tires squealed as I zoomed forward and then did a turn to face the back of this crazy bastard's car. I pulled my gun and trained my spotlight on his back window. I was on the mic pronto.

"10-33 request assistance, man with a gun, I'm at the Hilton."

From atop the parking garage, I could hear sirens coming to life from several different directions around the city. Bill was the first to get there. And within two minutes there were three more cars up the ramp. I went through the felony stop procedures, having him throw his keys out the window and open the door from the outside. He was wearing a leather jacket, and I didn't have him lift up his jacket to see if he was armed. He already told me he was, so it was as good as if I had seen it. I didn't want him to put his hands down to his body for any reason.

He complied with all our orders, and we got him handcuffed. Sure enough, this guy had a loaded 45 semi-automatic handgun in a shoulder holster. This guy in a calm voice said, "This used to be a nice neighborhood and now it's all niggers and Mexicans, so I want to die. I live right down on the street. I know you guys come up here to write your reports. My plan was to come up here and pull my gun so you guys would shoot me."

I took the guy in for 5150 Welfare and institutions code. If we feel someone is mentally ill and is a danger to themselves or others, this code gives us the authority to take them into custody and transport them to a mental health facility to be evaluated for a possible 72-hour observation. I transported him the Augustus Hawkins Medical Center. When I got him inside, a black attendant approached us. Oh man, the guy went nuts when he saw the attendant, yelling, "Nigger! Get this nigger away from me—don't let this nigger touch me!" He ended up in four-point restraints, and I never heard what happened to him after that.

We didn't park at the Hilton for a while. I talked with my friend Greg, a dispatcher at the East LA radio center. He was working our frequency that night. He said that one of the deputies was a detective working overtime in a patrol position. He radioed in, "Where's the Hilton, there's no Hilton in Lynwood." This guy kept hearing Lynwood units go 1097 arriving at the scene, and he was bewildered. Greg goes on ride alongs at every station, and he knew exactly where the Hilton was and directed him in. It was a good lesson, to be careful what you give a nickname to. Not everyone will know what you're talking about.

SAN DIEGO LICENSE PLATES

It was nice when we got computers in the cars. We could run license plates all night long. We no longer had to wait for the radio to be clear, which it never was. Now we could really be on the hunt for crooks and especially stolen cars. I was rolling south on Long Beach Blvd in the number two lane, and in front of me driving south was a pickup truck with a camper shell. The license plate frame read "San Diego." Oh man, San Diego license plate frames; that's almost an automatic stolen car.

I entered the plate into my computer as we continued south. Sure enough, the dispatcher came on the air.

"251 status regarding your 10-29 Victor (stolen car)." Yes!

"Give me the patch, I'm following a 10-29 Victor south on Long Beach Blvd approaching Compton."

As assisting units were coming, the stolen truck started making all sorts of turns. Finally, while we were stopped at the red light of El Segundo and Wilmington Avenue, tires started squealing and we were off to the races. I put out the pursuit. It's quite a wonderful, exciting thing being in pursuit: the rotating lights bouncing off the houses, siren blaring, sparks flying as the stolen vehicle bottoms out at a low spot in the road. I know, it's dangerous, but I miss it. I was having a ball, but this pursuit had gone on for a while. I don't know who the watch commander was, but bless him for letting this chase go on. When you're chasing a stolen car, if more information isn't revealed indicating it's more than a stolen car, the watch commander is required to cancel the pursuit. The amount of time the watch commander lets the pursuit go before he cancels it is subjective, so different watch commanders with different philosophies would handle things differently.

We got an air unit over the pursuit and assisting units behind me, and all of a sudden, the truck stopped. We took three in custody for the stolen truck. Sure enough, they had crossed the border and stolen the first vehicle they could so they could get to the city of angels. That's a pretty common scenario, which is why we were always on the lookout for San Diego license plate frames.

FIRST TRAINEE

I was picked to be a training officer. I wasn't sure if I wanted that job. It was a big responsibility, teaching and a lot of documentation. At the time, I didn't like reports. But if you ever want to get promoted to detective, become a sergeant, or go to a specialized unit, you have to have been a T/O to be considered for the job. My first trainee was Dani, and she was small in stature but tough as nails. She did a great job and did not take any shit from anybody.

Dani and I had a weird case that turned into a big lawsuit. The county ended paying out over $800,000. I hesitate too give out to many details as the memories of lengthy depositions flood my brain. Because it was such a newsworthy and noteworthy lawsuit, I choose to be brief in my description. We made a traffic stop and towed a vehicle. The occupant became hostile and refused to go with us to the station where they could be picked up. Dani took copious notes of our taking the driver to a safe location. Later the person claimed to have been assaulted, although the story given to another police agency didn't add up. A year later the person sees a wanted poster of a murder suspect and calls it in as the same person that assaulted them after we towed the car. Sure enough, the tattoos described in the police report matched the wanted poster. The person ended up being the only surviving witness who could identify the suspect and testify.

One night we had a car stopped on Atlantic Avenue in East Compton. We were searching for the car and had three male Hispanics in our backseat. We were standing between the car we had stopped and the patrol car, when Dani pointed to a car driving south on Atlantic. "That's the stolen car they just put out a broadcast on." We jumped in our patrol car, did a quick turn and got up on the stolen car within half a mile. We broadcast that we were behind the stolen car and requested assistance for a felony stop. Two cars quickly came up behind us, and we activated our overhead lights to initiate the traffic stop. And we were off.

The stolen car kicked up dust as it accelerated to a high rate of speed. We started broadcasting our pursuit. After a couple of quick turns off Atlantic Avenue onto some side streets, the doors flew open and two suspects were out of the car and on the run. We quickly set up a containment of the area and called for a k9 and Aero unit. We had the containment set up quick since we already had two assisting units behind us when we started our pursuit. If you get a good containment set up quick, you have a good chance of getting your crooks. The Watch Commander responded, and we briefed him on what was going on. I had a dry erase board on the hood of our car where I put the location of all of the units. We were standing around the hood of our patrol car. The Watch Commander said, "Everything looks good, but who are those guys?" pointing to our backseat. Oh shit, I forgot about the three male Hispanics we had in our backseat from the traffic stop we were on when we saw the stolen car go by. We quickly got them out of the car and sent them on their way walking back to their car still parked on Atlantic Avenue. Thankfully the Watch Commander was a veteran street cop and just laughed it off. He could have really jammed us up for taking our detainees on a high-speed chase.

The K9 unit arrived and found our two suspects in the containment. We took them into custody without incident or dog bite.

CARVER PARK MASSACRE 2

Dani and I were working the Willowbrook car on pm shift. We received a 415G call: a large gathering of gang members in Carver Park. It had been over a year since our original Carver Park massacre incident. Most of them knew me, and we had an understanding. Backup units were rolling but were quite a ways away. I thought we could roll in and handle this, put out a code 4 (no further assistance needed; all ok) and save the backup units the long roll. It was still daylight and a hot summer afternoon. We rolled into the park, and there must have been two hundred Crips in the park all dressed down in their blue dew rag gang attire. Everything looked calm, so I rolled up over the curb and drove into the center of the park on the grass. All of a sudden, a sea of gang members surrounded the Sheriff's Car. Oh shit, this turned real bad fucking fast.

Then some crazy-eyed bastard rushed up to my driver's door throwing gang signs yelling, "What's up my nigger, cmon nigger motherfucker—let's dance."

When I picked up the mic, everyone started running out of the park like mad. Crazy eyes started running away right in front of the police car. This crazy bastard had a handgun in the back of his waistband. I put out, "10-33 requesting assistance, man with a gun Carver Park." I must have had fifteen cars show up in less than five minutes. I couldn't figure out at the time why there were so many gang units out, marked and unmarked units. And some from other stations.

Later I found there had been a funeral for a Crip gang member shot and killed earlier in the week. I'll never forget the name, Diamond Blue. The gang units had wind of the funeral and the probable aftermath. These Carver Park Crips were all juiced up after the funeral having a good time until I showed up. We set up a containment, and we got crazy eyes. About 20 went to jail that day. Not quite as many as Carver Park massacre number 1. The gang unit knew crazy eyes and told me that he was a wannabe Crip gang member, and he pulled this stunt to gain favor with the gang. He was acting on his own.

HAM PARK

Ham Park, located in the northeast end of Lynwood was a park controlled by Young Crowd, a Hispanic gang. All over the northeast area of Lynwood you would see "YC" graffiti marking Young Crowd's area. The park looked like a normal park during the day. But at night, looks could be deceiving. It was not unusual for the pm shift to have a few drinks after shift. A little choir practice to unwind. Sometimes it was convenient to have choir practice at the rear of the station parking lot. Some higher up decided that city officials might see this in their comings and goings, as City Hall was right next door. So the order came down: no more drinking in the parking lot.

One night the pm shift picked Ham Park as a nice spot to get together after the end of shift. That was until Young Crowd did a drive-by on the deputies, who returned numerous rounds. No one was hit. I remember coming into the station on the early morning shift and seeing all the pm deputies and a sergeant writing reports. When they got shot at, more than a few deputies returned fire. Nobody was hit, but of course, there was a clusterfuck of paperwork to write.

P.M. Choir practice moved to a different park in the city. That didn't work: shot at again, return fire. Back to the station for more memos to the captain. A new order, no more choir practices in the city of Lynwood.

THE BUMPER JACK

The last night of training for my Trainee Eric Parra was a hot summer weekend night. Right after briefing before we went 10-8 in the field, I received a phone call from Eric's dad, who was a homicide detective. He said, "Thanks, Cliff. You did a great job with Eric. I really appreciate you taking care of him." Laughing, he said, "You didn't get him into a shooting, but I won't hold that against you." I jokingly told him the shift just started. We also had a station CSO with us as a ride along. CSO stands for civilian service officer, and they take minor reports like vandalism, and they write parking tickets. Many of them are too young to become deputies, but that is their ultimate goal. It was a wild night from the start, and the action didn't stop until the early morning hours. We were going call to call.

The crew from the TV show Cops were riding along with the gang units. We were assisting units in East Compton with an officer involved shooting. Deputies Ripley and Blackwell had got behind a stolen car. They were coordinating a felony stop when the passenger leaned out the car door and started shooting at the deputies with an AK- 47 assault rifle. The deputies seeing the barrels of the gun as it came out the window were able to lean down below the dashboard as numerous rounds smashed through the front windshield. Both the driver and passenger headrests were ripped apart by numerous rounds.

Both deputies came close to being killed that night, but luckily came out of it unscathed. They didn't get the vehicle that night, and I don't remember how but they identified the gang member who did the shooting. He was apprehended months later and is serving time for the attempted murder of a police officer. At the time, the AK-47—for the most part—was the weapon of choice in drive-by shootings. This was a Russian made military assault rifle that had a cyclic firing rate of 600 rounds per minute and was capable of both semiautomatic and automatic fire. It had a long curved box magazine that held 30 rounds.

We had to leave the scene and respond to a call of a gang fight at Tam's number nine, a popular food place on Long Beach Blvd at the

89

intersection of Josephine Avenue in the City of Lynwood. As we drove north on Long Beach Blvd still several hundred yards from Tam's, we saw two bodies run out into the street in front of the place, immediately followed by what looked like fifteen to twenty people. As we approached, it looked like they were all fighting with some kind of weapons. Eric barely got out, "Should we call it...?" before I just grabbed the mic and broadcasted, "10-33 requesting assistance Long Beach and Josephine in front of Tam's, 415 (disturbance/fight) twenty involved."

The crowd was fighting across both northbound lanes of Long Beach Blvd. As we came to a stop in the number two lane about ten yards from the crowd, I saw a male Hispanic take a big overhead swing and hit a guy in the back with what looked like a big sledge hammer. He dropped one guy and hit another. Eric and I both were out of our cars simultaneously. I remember Eric yelling, "Drop the Ax!" He thought it was an ax. In what seemed like a second, the male Hispanic was raising the metal sledgehammer over his head, in what I describe as a ring the bell move as you would see at a carnival. As it was raised over his head with his next target facing away from him engaged in a fight with someone else, I fired four shots as I stood straddling the number one and two lanes. I had no other alternative in an effort to protect the life of the person he was about to hit in the head. He then dropped what we later discovered was a bumper jack. Some of you may remember the old type bumper jacks which were long pieces of steel with a big metal head on it where you inserted the tire iron and put a protrusion under the lip of the bumper so you could raise the car to change a tire. In the dim light of streetlamps, it actually does look like an ax.

After dropping the bumper jack, he started running across the median into the southbound lanes of traffic. He then fell to the street, and I held him at gunpoint as I radioed in a 998 (officer-involved shooting) suspect down, no deputies injured. I requested 902R (rescue unit) and additional deputies because the gang members were still fighting. All this mayhem was taking place right in front of Tam's hamburger joint. I remember seeing the cooks inside flipping burgers and casually looking on as all this was going on. Gang fight, cops shooting, sirens, ambulances, and these guys never missed a beat cooking their food.

Deputies arrived, and Deputy Nordscog walked up to me and asked what happened, and I told him, "Well I shot this guy."

Nordscog said, "No."

The guy on the ground looking up at us said, "Yeah, he fucking shot me, and I'm the victim here." We found out later, he was kind of right. While we were standing in the street waiting for the ambulance, the scene got crazier. Deputies were making arrests, and some people were resisting. And then a car came screaming northbound, and to avoid hitting everyone in the street it went up onto the median and hit a tree at about 30 miles per hour. That driver got arrested for drunk driving, and he was hammered out of his mind.

Eric was worried. His dad at Homicide was next on call. Considering the conversation his dad and I had after the briefing, he passed it on to the next team.

Finally, everything got settled down. People went to jail. The crime scene was secured for Homicide and the shooting team to come out and do their investigation. Homicide comes out on all hit shootings, and this is how it was in 1989. Witnesses were secured at the station awaiting for Homicide to finish with the scene and come to the station for the interviews.

I felt a little bad that the guy I shot was a member of the armed forces. He fully recovered, and no lawsuit followed. He and his buddy had been on a ship or otherwise deployed at some remote assignment for six months. They went on leave and were shortly at Tam's number nine to order some food. They were waiting for their food when two attractive young Hispanic girls came in to order food. The two servicemen started catcalling them, saying, "I would love to fuck that."

The girls said, "Oh yeah, we will see about that." The girls left and returned a couple of minutes later with about fifteen local gang members. The two servicemen saw the gang coming and ran to their car where they armed themselves with the bumper jack and a tire iron. Severely outnumbered, they ran into the street where they were quickly surrounded. This is what we saw as we were driving north on Long Beach approaching the scene. One marine started swinging the bumper jack while the other was swinging the tire iron trying to fight off the attacking gang members in Custard's Last Stand fashion. The gang members were glad the service guy got shot. One of the rare occasions that fifteen gang members gave witness statements that were consistent with and supported the police accounts of what happened. For many years after that, Tam's would be known as the bumper jack. It was funny to hear on the radio years later, "Where ya wanna eat, the bumper jack?"

Eric passed field training with flying colors and climbed the ranks reaching Commander.

MY GLASSES FLEW OFF

It wasn't too long after Blackwell and Ripley survived the shooting in East Compton that Blackwell and I were working together. We had a great time working together. Gary Blackwell was another deputy I had the privilege to work with. A genuine, good guy. We were working the midnight shift (early morning shift), and at about 1 am we were driving behind a van on San Fernando Road near the Watts Towers. The van was swerving all over the place, crossing the center lines. Both Blackwell and I said to each other that we had to stop this guy. We activated the overhead lights, and no reaction. The van continued on San Fernando road. As we crossed the boundary line from the county area of L.A. to the City of L.A., we hit the siren.

Still no reaction. I felt Gary tense up in the passenger seat next to me. It had just been a few weeks since he was the passenger officer with Ripley, and the passenger in the stolen car they were trying to stop let loose with a barrage of bullets into their front windshield, nearly killing them both. I'm sure he was feeling a little deja vu. He later told me that he was thinking, Oh shit, here we go again.

We were about to broadcast that we were in pursuit when the van suddenly came to a stop. The driver didn't pull to the side of the road, just stopped in the lane. We should have asked for backup, but instead we had another unit go to a tactical frequency, and we told deputy Chavez about our stop. We told him something didn't feel right and to start heading our way. Luckily the lieutenant and some other units were monitoring the frequency, and hearing the tone of our voices, started to roll to our location.

I approached the driver while Blackwell approached the passenger side of the van. It was a panel van with no side windows. Blackwell and I couldn't see each other until we got across from each other at the front seat of the van. I asked the black male driver for his driver's license and registration to the vehicle. He started pounding both fists on the steering wheel, staring straight ahead yelling, "I don't have a fucking license!" It was a pretty cool night, and he was in a white t-shirt soaked in sweat. I tried to talk to him in a calming voice. I told him it was no problem and asked him if he had any identification. He continued staring straight ahead, pounding on the steering wheel again yelling, "I don't have any fucking I. D!"

I asked him to step out of the van, and he complied. I directed him to the hood of our patrol car. As I had him put his hands on the front hood of our car so I could search him, deputy Chavez arrived and was walking toward the front of our patrol car. Just as I started patting down our suspect, he wheeled around and threw a punch at my face. I jerked my head around and avoided the punch, but my glasses flew off and landed in the street. Chavez, Blackwell and I took the suspect to the ground. He would not submit to arrest, and the fight was on. I was able to get to my handheld radio and broadcast, "10-33 requesting assistance deputies involved in a fight San Fernando Road near the Watts Towers." We were rolling around on the ground and couldn't get this guy's arms behind his back for handcuffing. He was so slippery because of his sweat and had abnormal strength.

Seemed like just a minute since I asked for help when Lt. Jackson rolled up and asked, "Is it code-4?" I told him no, we need more help. This guy has to be on PCP. The field lieutenant was now out of his car and in the fight with us. He tipped the scales in our favor, and we were able to get him handcuffed. He had all the symptoms of someone under the influence of PCP, and that's what we arrested him for. He would have to be taken to a hospital and be approved for booking. And the only hospital that would take people under the influence of PCP was MLK (Martin Luther King). Lieutenant Jackson told me that when he heard my voice over L-Tac that he knew something was wrong, and he started heading in our direction.

I always appreciate Lt. Jackson for rolling to our backup. I never forgot that, and we were always friendly for years after that. We later worked together at West Hollywood Station and always had great conversations. I make mention of him backing us up because when he first arrived at Lynwood station as a Lieutenant, he gave a briefing and laid down the law as to what he expected. It was not well received by some of the deputies. One early morning shift, he stopped a guy in an alley who he searched and found had a gun. He asked for backup, and no one responded. I was not working when this happened. Maybe nobody heard his broadcast. If I had heard his request, it would not have been in my DNA not to back him up. Even though he had that experience, he was there when I asked for back up.

After booking our PCP suspect, we never heard about our case again until about two years later. Blackwell and I were named as defendants in a Federal Civil Rights violation trial. I had already been transferred from the station when the lawsuit came down. We were accused of beating him and not taking him for immediate medical attention. We got to the trial, and Blackwell and I sat at the defendants' table with our county attorneys as if we committed a crime. We arrested him for being under the influence of PCP. His blood sample came back as being under the influence of cocaine. The Judge said since we didn't charge him with being under the influence of cocaine, the Jury couldn't be told this. So we had to testify that we arrested him for being under the influence of PCP. The attorney asked, "And did he test positive for PCP?" and when we said no, the attorney said, "No further questions."

The Jury never knew that he was high as a kite on cocaine. Then they advised the Jury that a hospital was a half-mile away, but we took him three miles to another hospital because we didn't want him to have immediate medical attention. Because he didn't test positive for PCP, our attorney was not allowed to explain to the Jury we had to take him to the other hospital because it was the only hospital that will take patients under the influence of PCP.

I almost burst out laughing when Deputy Chavez was testifying while he was explaining how as he was walking toward our patrol car, he saw the suspect attempt to punch me in the face, and I turned my head to avoid the punch. The attorney asked Chavez what he saw next, and Cavez stated, "Yates' glasses flew off, landing in the street." I almost started laughing because as he said my glasses flew off, he gave me a brief look that said to me, See how I got the part about your glasses falling off in. You have to know Deputy Chavez, he was a great cop, and when he testified, he painted a picture that made you feel like you were right there with him as it was happening.

I couldn't believe the legal arguments between the attorneys and the federal Judge not in the presence of the Jury. When they wanted to make a legal argument, they would have the Jury escorted out of the courtroom. The attorneys admitted that their client was high on cocaine and drove his van to south central L.A. to buy more drugs, and that's when we pulled him over. Since we didn't charge him with being under the influence of cocaine, the attorney requested that the Jury not be told that. The Judge agreed, so the Jury never knew that he was high on coke. They only got to hear that we arrested him for being under the influence of PCP, and a blood test showed that we wasn't. These attorneys did what they call "buy the medical bills." He was in custody, so his medical treatment was paid for by the county. So they reimbursed the county, so they could show they were suing for the cost of the medical bills. That way if they were awarded one dollar, their attorney fees were covered — what a system.

We were found to have violated his civil rights, but the Judge ruled no punitive damages. Meaning we didn't have to pay, just the county.

NEW TRAINEE

I got a new trainee, big Tim Anderson. He was a giant of a man, about 6'2 260lbs, mostly muscle. He had a powerlifter physique. Tim was having a bad day. It was one of those Lynwood overwhelming days. We were finishing our fourth booking of the day, and Tim was backed up on reports. I told him to do something, and he barked back at me, "You do it."

Now I was a bit of a different person at this time in my life. I went off on Tim. I was yelling, "Me do it? Come here, fucker." I directed him into a room. "Sit the fuck down and wait here for me!" I yelled, slamming the door. This room had a bunch of booking forms in it, and it doubled as a juvenile detention room. So I knew when I shut the door, there was no door handle on the inside; someone has to let you out. I went to the Watch Sergeant, who was a tough lady with many years of experience. She was old school. I told her what happened with Anderson, and she asked me where he was. I pointed to the detention room. "He's in there. The door is shut so he can't get out."

She said, "Fuck him, leave him in there a while until he has a better attitude."

I walked by the dispatch area about an hour later, and Tim was standing at the door window of the detention room, sheepishly knocking on the door. I think he needed to go to the bathroom. I let him out, and we had a talk. He had a change in attitude, and we ended up great friends after he got off training. Tim was a good cop. He did well at Lynwood and later transferred to Santa Clarita Station to be closer to home. Just a couple years later, Tim developed some type of intestinal cancer and passed away. I still think of some of the great times we had working together. We, like so many great deputies I worked with, had some great laughs together.

ROBBERY SUSPECT SHOOTING

Tim Anderson and I were working a pm shift. I was driving, and he was in his last month of training. It was just about dark when we got behind a black Lincoln Continental on El Segundo Blvd and stopped at a red light at the intersection of Willowbrook Avenue. The Lincoln suddenly made a right turn on to Willowbrook Avenue against the red light. I told Tim, "Here we go." Before I could get the red lights on to conduct a traffic stop, the chase was on. Dust was kicking up on to our windshield as the hotrod Lincoln kicked in high gear. Tim called in that we were in pursuit. I didn't know what we had. I'm sure I said it was a suspected stolen car.

As we skidded right on to 130th Street from Wilmington Avenue, the passenger started tossing items out of the window. He got close to 100 mph as we passed Aranbe Avenue. He tried to hit the brakes, but he was never going to make it past the T intersection of Wilmington Avenue. He didn't make it crossing Wilmington Avenue, striking a light pole at the median. All four doors of the Lincoln flew open, and four male blacks were out in a flash. Tim and I were out with our guns drawn at a position of cover behind our car doors. In my field of vision, everything was a blur except a small square of the driver's left arm and shoulder. As he got out of the driver's door and started running, he began turning, and I saw the barrel of a small handgun in his hand. He was facing forward as his arm was swinging back toward me. I fired three quick shots. In a flash, the driver and left rear passenger were running straight across Wilmington Avenue into a field out of view. We approached the car to clear it of any additional suspects. As Tim got to the front passenger door, he yelled, "You got this one!"

I was thinking, What the fuck, I better have not gotten that one, I was never shooting in that direction. I didn't even see the suspect on the passenger side. Turned out the guy on the passenger side heard the shots, decided to give up, and just laid down on the ground. I said, "Jesus Tim, you scared the shit out of me."

Tim said, "I didn't know. I heard you shoot, and this guy right away fell to the ground." The suspects had ran across Wilmington Avenue into the school grounds of Willowbrook Middle School. We immediately set up a containment and called for an airship and K-9. The Watch Commander rolled out to the scene. He didn't have it out for me, but I know he wasn't my biggest fan. Since it appeared it was a non-hit shooting, he had the handle. If it had been a hit shooting, homicide and the shooting team would roll and have the handle. The Commander was probably a little miffed he had this shooting on his watch, and probably a lot of pissed because it was a non-hit he had to handle. A pursuit, terminating in a TC (traffic collision) and a shooting, was going to be a nightmare of paperwork. The rest of the shift was happy.

This meant that for the next week or so, the Watch Commander would not have time to be snooping into anyone's business until he had this investigation completed. I know I saw a gun, but the pissed off Watch Commander is thinking, Everyone was running, you shot, and you said you saw a gun to cover the shooting. Since everyone fled on foot, he could make that assertion. Thankfully not too long after, my observation would be substantiated.

The containment was in place, aero unit overhead and K9 unit was on the way. The Lincoln came back stolen from the city of Gardenia and used in an armed robbery. We transported the one suspect to the station to book him on the stolen car and robbery charge. While at the station, another unit arrived to book a suspect that the K9 unit captured. And the suspect hiding in a field could have disposed of all evidence that he was involved in a crime, but he didn't. He still had the gun and a watch that was taken in the armed robbery in his pants pocket. My observation of the gun was substantiated. I was sure the driver was going to plug me in the head as he ran from the car. It was another good night working the streets, chasing bad guys, catching them, recovering stolen items, and taking a gun off the street.

ASSAULT WITH A DOG

I was between trainees, and my good friend and classmate was working alone monitoring one of her trainees who was working a one-man car. She was acting as his sister car. She was tough as they come, and she didn't take shit from anyone. She was a great police officer and went on after Lynwood station to a long career in the department. She was a female officer that I trusted with my life. She worked harder than anyone else.

Her trainee received a disturbance call. I responded to back them up. We arrived before her trainee. As we parked in front, we saw a large male Hispanic hitting a heavy bag hanging in his garage. My classmate said her trainee was taking too long and said, "Let's contact this guy."

We called for the guy to come out of the garage and come talk to us on the driveway. We were standing in the long driveway, about 20 yards from the garage. Boxer Boy yelled back, "Get the fuck outta here, and take the nigger bitch with you!" Oh shit, I could tell my partner was pissed. Just outside the garage, there was a doghouse with a pit boxer mix that was on a chain barking like mad. Boxer Boy said, "You want me to come out there? Ok." He grabbed the pit boxer and took him off the leash. He put the dog between his legs facing us as he held the dog by his head with just the hind legs on the ground. He began walking toward us, stopping every couple feet, holding the dog's head with one hand while he simultaneously slapped the side of the dog's head. He continued to do this, switching hands and continuing to slap the side of the dog's head hard. Then he would squeeze the side of the dog's cheeks. He was working this dog up hard. He was growling and frothing at the mouth, and Boxer Boy continued toward us.

I pulled my gun and stepped back a couple of steps. I was really mad that this guy might put us in a position of hurting the dog. I love animals, and the sight of him slapping the dog was really pissing me off. My partner pulled her gun and stepped forward, yelling at the guy, "Put the dog back on the fucking leash now!"

He yelled back, "Get off my property nigger bitch, or I'm letting the dog go to rip you to shit!"

She moved forward, telling the guy, "You are going to jail."

I pointed my gun straight out and started walking forward. I was for backing up and giving us some time in case he lets the dog go, but my partner was marching forward and in advance mode. So, I was in. I had my gun hand outstretched, and now we are about 20 feet from the guy and the dog. He was continuing to slap the dog in the head and work him up into more of a frenzy, if that was possible. I wanted to try and scare this guy into giving up, so I yelled to my partner, "If he lets the dog go, I'm shooting this guy in the head. You kill the dog." I said this as a ruse, in an attempt to get him to give up. I think it worked a little.

Now the guy started backing up with the dog, still slapping the shit out of him. He backs himself to a side gate attached to the garage. We had maintained a distance of about 20 feet. He continued to hold on to the pit boxer while he reached back with one hand, unlatched the gate and yelled, "Getem!" Out of the yard comes this charging pitbull, running full throttle locked in on me. I fired four shots in rapid succession. That pitbull skidded headfirst to a dead stop right at my feet. When I say dead stop, I mean he was dead. Four shots right to the head. Now I'm in kill mode.

This guy yells, "You shot my dog!"

I'm yelling, "Let the other one go, and he's next. Come on you pussy, let him go!"

He says, "No, you're going to shoot him." He puts the dog back on the leash and gets down on the ground and submits to arrest without further incident.

I was so pissed he put us in a position where we had to shoot the pit bull. I really felt bad about killing the dog. I was so pissed at this son of a bitch causing his dog to be shot. If I had been forced to shoot and kill Boxer Boy, believe me, I wouldn't have felt bad at all. Killing the dog really bothered me. I love animals. I had been bitten before on the job, and boy they can get to you fast.

Boxer Boy was charged with two counts of 245pc, assault on a peace officer with a deadly weapon. The D.A. filed two counts because he used both dogs as a weapon. He was convicted on both counts and served four years in prison. When we arrested him, he was on parole for a previous assault charge. Mom had been slapped around by him and was happy when we took him away. My classmate's trainee never made it to the call. I imagine he wishes he had after my partner got through with him.

STEVE BLAIR

I was frequently partnered with Steve Blair. I think we had been partnered together a couple of times, and we had so much fun that we started signing up for overtime together. We had so many laughs. People say I'm funny. I thought Steve was a funny bastard. I was with him on some call where an ambulance was needed. I remember that's where Steve first met Dana, who ended up being the love of his life, and not long after they were married.

I was transferred out of Lynwood in 1991. Steven went on to the gang unit and still worked in the Lynwood area. In May of 1995, he was patrolling on Walnut Avenue next to Ham Park. He stopped to check two gang members. As he got out of his car, he was shot and killed. The gang member was captured and convicted, sentenced to death. I went to several officer funerals after that, and Dana was always there sitting near me, holding Steve's Lynwood jacket. Seeing Dana holding his jacket with tears in her eyes was always a knife to the heart.

LYNWOOD VIKINGS

When we as a group of trainees first arrived at Lynwood Station and went to the orientation, we were all given a Lynwood Viking Pin to wear on our uniforms. A Viking flag hung on the briefing wall. Most stations had a mascot. Lennox had the grim reaper, and Lakewood the Sea Hawk.

In my last month of training, Marv said that I would probably be approached to get a Viking tattoo. He said I would have to make up my own mind whether to get it or not. He said that a group of deputies who were no longer at the station had been involved in misconduct that were attributed to a group who had the tattoos. He said the idea behind the tattoo was camaraderie amongst hard-charging deputies, but some bad apples had changed the perception of some of the higher-ups in the department. Long before I got there, he told me a deputy who used to be a station secretary put the captain's personal license into the system as stolen. Someone allegedly sent a hearse to an executive's house. All this activity was before I got to the station.

I had been at the station for almost three years when the captain started giving interviews with a reporter from the Long Beach Press paper. All of a sudden there were newspaper articles where the captain mentioned numerous incidents of misconduct, and that there was a segment at the station that was too closely associated to the Viking mascot which the community feels is representative of a blonde hair, raping and pillaging marauder. The captain said the element at the station is like cancer and needed to be cut out. He made it sound like the misconduct from previous years involved current personnel at the station. He then ordered that the Viking would no longer be the station mascot. This was met with immediate pushback.

Deputies from all over the county were hired for overtime to work the Rose Parade in Pasadena. The Pasadena Police Chief told the Sheriff he did not want any deputies working the parade from the Lynwood station due to what was in the recent articles.

Then in 1991 five deputies, myself included, were advised that we were being transferred out of the station. None of us wanted to be transferred. We sued to stop the transfers, but a judge would not issue an injunction to stop the transfer pending a hearing. The department said it was not punitive, and that we were being transferred to premium positions and/or stations. We were all transferred to what would be considered choice assignments. The problem in our view was that in lieu of what was said in the newspaper articles, our transfers would link us as deputies that had been involved in misconduct, and we were the cancer that needed to be cut out. I had not served a day of suspension since being on the department. We knew that other department members would look at our transfers as an indication of our involvement in misconduct.

"Oh your those troublemakers from Lynwood."

Deputies amongst themselves decided to choose fellow deputies who they felt were hard workers and did great police work to be deserving of the station tattoo. Many of the deputies were Hispanic, and there were some black deputies and some female. Unfortunately, if you google Lynwood Viking, you will find search results indicating a white supremacist police gang. This was blatantly not true.

When we filed suit, our names were on the front page of the L.A. Metro section: "Five deputies sue Sheriff over transfers." Since we didn't get an injunction to stop the transfers and winning our suit would have just allowed us to go back to Lynwood, we all decided to drop the suit. We were not seeking any money, just to stay at Lynwood. If we won it might have been years later, and by then we wouldn't want to go back. In the end, it was the best thing for all of us. But not in the short term. I was an aggressive type-A personality: kind of a hothead at the time. Looking back, I should have been thankful for the transfer.

I was approached by supervisors at the time who liked me and wanted to tell me how this was going to be good for me. I regret at the time I was not receptive to any input from these supervisors who as I look back on it were trying to be of help to me.

Many of us felt the brunt of retribution from supervisors who were against us for filing suit. I had a lieutenant corner me in the station parking lot. "You think you can sue the Sheriff and get away with it. We will never forget, and we're gonna get you." I felt negative repercussions to my career for about 7 or 8 years. Many Lynwood station deputies gave depositions in support of our suit. The five of us were transferred to choice patrol stations I believe in an effort to show that the transfers were not punitive. The deputies who gave depositions in our favor would not be so lucky. About a year after our transfers, Lynwood Station deputies were in a giant pursuit which ended in an officer-involved shooting. The department discovered that most of the deputies who gave depositions in our lawsuit were involved in this pursuit. They used the pursuit as an opportunity to transfer those deputies, and most were sent back to custody. The deputies that came out in support of us really got a kick in the teeth.

In 1998 Sheriff Block passed away, and there was a new Sheriff in town. About ten years after our lawsuit, all was mostly forgotten, and things started to turn around for me. In reality, it was when I changed that things began to change for the positive. As I had to discover for myself, it's never them, the economy, the circumstances; the problem was an inside job. I was the problem. I had little control over what happened to me. I had one hundred percent control of how I reacted to it. I wasn't quite ready for that lesson.

WALNUT STATION

I didn't want to be transferred, and I especially didn't want to be transferred to Walnut Station. It was considered a slow station that you went to when you wanted to ride out the rest of your time until retirement. But it was a giant station that had San Dimas sub-station. I spent the next four years there. It was different, more than slow. My first year at the station, there were ten officer-involved shootings. So much for slow. Besides a huge county area, Walnut had the contract cities of Walnut, Diamond Bar and San Dimas. The station also deployed mountain cars, and a mountain rescue unit. When I arrived at Walnut, there were about five other deputies who had been transferred in under a cloud. The Captain met with us and said we were starting with a clean slate, and he meant it.

I was transferred to Walnut Station around January 1991, and in April of 1992 in response to the LAPD Officer verdict in the Rodney King case, the L.A. Riots started. The LAPD had started preparation for reaction to the verdicts if they went in the officer's favor. They didn't plan for and could not have anticipated the degree to which the civil unrest escalated. Most of the initial unrest and violence started in south-central L.A. in LAPD's area. But it quickly spread all over south L.A.

A year after being transferred out of Lynwood Station I found myself as part of a response team being sent back to the area in response to the riots. From Walnut we sent about ten cars each with four deputies in riot gear. We had a lieutenant and one or two sergeants. We had our helmets, riot batons, tear gas, ballistic shields and all the rest that goes with riot gear. We spent most of our time in ready mode stationed behind strip malls, and when the need came for a response team, we would be called into action and deploy as a squad to wherever the trouble was. Most of our deployments involved moving and dispersing large crowds. Although the department had mobile booking trailers and some response teams made numerous arrests, ours was not one of them. The riots comprised about six days of violence. After the six days, we went from being on 12-hour shifts back to our station and normal schedules.

One thing the L.A. County Sheriff's Department does extremely well is operate the Emergency Operation Canter. Each station is equipped to operate its own Emergency Operation Center. In any major incident, the department is able to send a response force quickly. Each station on every shift has designated units for an emergency response team. Each station usually has between ten and twenty deputies designated for the response team. With over twenty patrol stations in the county that equates to over 400 deputies that can quickly be deployed to any location. If need be, the jail division can have over 500 deputies deployed as an emergency response team. Many of the deputies from the jail are not patrol trained, but they are well trained in crowd control, squad formations, riot training, and deployment of special weapons.

In 1993 major fires started burning in Malibu. This fire quickly started burning out of control. I was on the emergency response team from Walnut Station. We sent about ten cars with three to four deputies to each car. We headed down the freeway caravanning with our lights and sirens blaring in route to Malibu. We left Walnut Station in bright sunshine. We arrived at the command post at the old Malibu Sheriff's Station just off PCH (Pacific Coast Highway). When we left Santa Monica travailing south on PCH, we went from bright sunshine to complete darkness. This was the middle of the day, and the smoke was so dark and thick, it completely blocked out the sun. Flames along the highway were leaping 200 feet in the air. Thank goodness for the goggles we were issued to protect our eyes. At the time, I was wearing hard contact lenses, and just a piece of dust could cause great pain and watering to my eyes.

We got out of our patrol cars, and the wind caused by the fires was really strong. Dust dirt and embers were flying everywhere. We were given our assignments and sent into areas to warn residents about the fires and advise them to evacuate. I can't remember if it was a mandatory evacuation or not. I do know that most did not leave. Some were downright hostile to our recommendation to evacuate. I remember people saying, "We have been through this before, we know better than you how to handle these fires." This fire was particularly dangerous in that most of the areas burning had not burned since the 1930s.

At the end of your shift, you were covered with smoke and smelled like a chimney. You get home after not having breathed in fresh air for over twelve hours. I think I responded to Malibu for several days in a row before returning to a normal patrol schedule.

In January of 1994 the Northridge earthquake hit, creating chaos in the San Fernando Valley and Santa Clarita. Again the station was put on 12 hours on, 12 hours off. Damage to the freeways cut the north end of the county off from the south end. Santa Clarita had widespread damage to homes and businesses. I was assigned to a response team deployed to Santa Clarita to provide patrols of neighborhoods and protect homes from looters. The problem was getting from Walnut to Santa Clarita. About forty of us were loaded into one of those big military Chinook helicopters. That was quite the experience.

We loaded up on a football field in Walnut. Then we were flown to the Magic Mountain amusement park in Valencia. When we got out of the helicopter, there were twenty marked patrol cars lined up waiting for us. Each of our two-person patrol teams went to our assigned radio cars and started our patrol shift. We were given maps and contact information. We had all of the Santa Clarita Station information and local court information for citations. We had booking kits all set up to help us book prisoners at Santa Clarita Station if needed. At the end of our shift, we would gas the car up and drive back to Magic Mountain and get back on a helicopter to be flown back to Walnut Station. The next team exited the helicopter and started their shift. It was a pretty well run operation. The amount of damage to all the homes was really shocking. Very sad to see all the people that were displaced from their homes.

Twenty-five years later and the earthquakes and devastation of 1994 are a distant memory. Santa Clarita has boomed in the years that followed and is prime real estate now.

* * *

At Walnut I worked with a partner, Joe Lomonaco. I never met anyone with more of a can-do attitude than he had. One thing he also had was an addiction to Skittles. Wherever we went, he had his Skittles. Before we went 10-8 in the field, we checked our car, guns, equipment and Joe's supply of Skittles.

We worked Rowland Heights, a county area that was predominantly Hispanic and Asian, but mostly Asian. The Asian restaurants were getting robbed at gunpoint on a regular basis. Asian gangs were a violent and active problem. Joe had worked Lakewood Station where they had tracker cars for money the bank kept which had a metal chip in it. When it was pulled from the drawer, the spring metal clips would contact each other and activate the chip. The track cars had boxes on the dashboard which would indicate with arrows the direction these chips were transmitting from so you could home in on the location of the money after it was taken from the bank. They also had these packs the size of a pack of cigarettes. They had a mercury bubble inside; when they were moved, they activated and sent a signal to the tracker cars.

Joe had a great idea. He said we could loan two Walnut cars to Lakewood in exchange for two-tracker cars. We could then put the packs and money in the Asian restaurants and catch the robbers in the act. These robberies were happening two or three times a week. Joe went to the Rowland Heights team leader deputy. He told the deputy he could write up the proposal, submit it, and take credit since he was the team leader for the area. The team leader told Joe he was nuts and that it would never be approved. He said he wasn't going to waste his time even proposing it. Joe asked the team leader if he could go ahead and try and get it done. He told Joe to go ahead.

Joe went to the Captain and proposed the idea. The Captain was all for it. But he didn't understand how the logistics of the car exchange would work. Joe said he knew the parties that had to be contacted in order to get it done. The Captain gave him the go-ahead, saying, "If you can make it happen, you have the approval on my end."

Joe made it happen. We did the car exchange and set out to distribute the packs that we put in purses to have the restaurant owners put behind the counter. During these robberies not only were they taking the money out of the registers, they were stealing the purses behind the counter that were usually left there by the hostess or the owner of the restaurant. At the beginning of the shift, we would go to our target restaurants, set up the registers and place the purses. We had enough purse packs and bait money for three restaurants. So, we would rotate the locations based on our best guess of where we thought the robbers might hit next. At the end of the shift, we would go back to the restaurants to pick up our wares.

So, picture how this looks to people sitting in the restaurant having dinner. Two deputies walk in just before closing. The owner walks to the register, opens it and takes out money and hands it to uniformed deputies. Then reaches behind the counter and hands us a purse, and we walk out. People must have thought we were the dirtiest deputies they ever saw. We tried to go as late as possible or after the restaurant closed. But we were usually getting off at 10 pm, and many times these restaurants still had patrons inside.

The team leader deputy was pissed off that Joe had made this happen. As if Joe had never gone to him and tried to let him have the credit for putting the operation together. Joe and I just wanted to catch the bad guys. Joe didn't care about getting the credit. This team leader guy never thought Joe could get it done, but he did. And man that guy was sour over it.

We had a few mishaps with our bait money. Several times the alarm would go off in the tracker box. Something about that noise going off and the direction signal blinking got your blood going. Ultimately the tracker led us to the restaurant, and the owner would apologize either for moving the bait purse or pulling out the bait money by mistake. Us coming through the front door with guns drawn was enough to make sure that didn't happen twice.

Eventually, the trackers got the robbers. Unfortunately, Joe and I were off, and two other deputies were able to take them down.

Working Rowland Heights with Joe was a blast. We laughed our asses off on a daily basis. And he was a great cop. We made some good hooks. Joe ended up going to a different shift, and I did too. I had an opportunity to become a team member at the San Dimas Substation. Being a team member deputy meant that I would always be assigned out of the San Dimas station and not be bounced around based on vacancies in other patrol positions. If you were not a core member of a contract city or permanent car, you could find yourself working out of the Walnut station one day and the next day out of the sub-station. I was assigned a traffic car. Most deputies never want to work in a traffic car. I liked it. You had to handle accidents, but the rest of your day was self-initiated activity. San Dimas was a great little city. They loved the Sheriff's Department and contracted with plenty of crime and traffic cars. Some cities would run a little short. San Dimas always had good coverage.

When I transferred to Walnut Station around January of 1991, I moved in with a deputy friend, Bill Costleigh. We lived in a condo at 1277 Sunflower Avenue, Covina about half a mile from the city limits of San Dimas. I joined the Bulldog Gym, which was just around the corner from our condo on Arrow highway just west of Sunflower Avenue. The gym was owned by a retired West Covina police officer. Most of the members were either law enforcement or firefighters, or the type that would support either.

One afternoon in 1995, I was working a traffic car in the City of San Dimas, and I pulled over a pick-up truck for speeding. The driver said his name was Louie Pompei, and he was a Glendora Police Officer. He said he recognized me from the Bulldog Gym. I recognized his passenger as a dispatcher from the Walnut Station, and she told me that Louie was engaged to her sister. After that day, I would see Louie in the gym on a regular basis. One day I saw a tattoo on his leg, and he told me he got it in Rochester, NY while he was in the service. Being from the Rochester area, we bonded and worked out together quite often. He and his fiancée lived in San Dimas in my patrol area. During my shift, I would stop in and visit Louis and his fiancée.

One day at the gym, I gave Louie a videotape of one of my stand-up comedy performances. The next time he saw me, he told me he laughed and laughed while watching the tape. He made me promise to invite him to my next performance. I told him I was going to a comedy seminar at Big Bear Mountain, where I would be learning how to promote my own shows, and that I would make sure he was at my first production.

On June 1st of 1995, I began working a temporary assignment at the Lost Hills/Malibu Station. Every summer, they have a large team that works strictly at the beach. I didn't get to work the beach team, but it was a nice change working the coast. So for three months, I would not be working at San Dimas Station.

On June 10th I was driving home from Big Bear Mountain, where I had attended that comedy seminar I had told Louis about. I was driving down the mountain in great spirits, when I got a phone call from a friend. He told me that Louie was shot and killed the night before in San Dimas.

Louie, his fiancée, and her sister had gone to Mexico and returned late to San Dimas. Louie at this time was assigned to a multi-jurisdictional drug task force, undercover. Louie went to the Vons supermarket to buy some dog food. While waiting in line to pay, a gang member pulled out a gun and ordered everyone to get on the floor. Louis was caught in the middle of a robbery in progress. He initially complied with the gang member's orders along with everyone else. When the gang member started pistol-whipping a clerk, Louis was compelled to intervene. He had no way of knowing; there was an accomplice standing behind him. When Louis intervened, the second gang member began shooting Louis in the back. Louie was able to wound two of the suspects and get to a pay phone in front of the store to dial 911.

Louie died of his gunshot wounds. Two suspects were arrested at a nearby hospital, and a third suspect was later arrested. Two of the juvenile suspects were convicted as adults of murdering a police officer, receiving life sentences. The third suspect was convicted and received 26 years.

At the service, I learned so much about Louie. So many people came. He was a devout Christian who had touched the lives of so many people with all of his good deeds, on and off duty. His dream was to be hired by the Los Angeles County Sheriff's Department. When he didn't get hired by the Sheriff's Department, he joined the Glendora Police Department.

The junction of the 57 freeway and the 210 freeway was a memorial interchange, with signs indicating it is a memorial interchange dedicated to Glendora Police Officer Louie Pompei. Whenever I drive to Los Angeles from my home in La Verne, I pass these signs dedicated to Louie. When I do, I always remember my good friend. Sometimes I even give him a salute and tell him that I will always remember him. Please read about Louis at the Officer Down Memorial Page.

SAN DIMAS STATION

I would spend the rest of my assigned time at Walnut Station working as a San Dimas Station team member. This is a memoir about my life as a cop, so I have purposely left out my love life trials and tribulations. But San Dimas is where I met my wife, who was working as a deputy out of Walnut. We met at the station in 1994 and started dating in 1995. We were married in 2002 and are still happily together today.

Here I was suing, trying not to get out of Lynwood, and was so devastated when that didn't happen. I would never have met my love had I not been transferred. I often think of that song by Garth Brooks, and sometimes I thank God for unanswered prayers.

There were many good times and blessings after being transferred to Walnut Station. But not too long after being transferred, I really went into a negative place. I was really pissed off and carried a lot of anger after the transfer. A lieutenant that had worked Lynwood transferred into Walnut Station, and he went after me big time. I had a complaint from a traffic stop I conducted and issued a ticket. The sergeant called me by phone to tell me about the complaint. I told him I had the entire contact on tape. He was surprised, saying, "You do? Let me hear the tape." I played the tape for him, and he said, "Oh, don't worry about it. I'll tell the Watch Commander." He called me back and said, "I don't know what to tell you, he said he is still writing you up for discourtesy." I grieved it and had two sergeants hear me out, and I never heard anything more, so I thought it was over.

Later I found out that the lieutenant put the writeup in my file as being discourteous. This same lieutenant called one of my partners in. He worked a sister car on my shift. He told my good friend to stay away from me, that I was a negative influence. He told my friend that I would drag his career down. My friend left his office and immediately told me of the conversation. This lieutenant had dated the same female deputy that I had dated, and I have to think that was part of his motivation. In retrospect, I was in a negative place, but that doesn't justify the way he went after me. But soon I would be turning things

115

around and not blaming anyone but myself for my circumstances. Our attitudes, philosophies, and beliefs are all an inside job. It's not circumstances. It's how we respond to them that matters.

I don't know how I got started into real estate, but I did. I got my real estate license and started going to sales training classes. I went to a seminar by Jim Rohn, who was the original teacher of Tony Robbins. I didn't even know there was a self-development, personal growth, motivational industry. I'm sure I read over 50 books on motivation and psychology. I read many of these books two and three times. When I changed, things began to change for me. All the skills that you learn in becoming a great real estate salesperson translates to the rest of your life. The power of a positive attitude was working in me every day. I was motivated to become a real estate agent and quit the Sheriff's Department. But as I grew as a person, I began becoming more successful at the department.

In 1993 one of my self-help motivational books was by Tony Robbins, Awaken The Giant Within. This got me going and motivated to a new level. I read another book by Tony, Unlimited Power. I also took his 30-day cassette course. One of my good friends from NY came out to visit after a breakup, and I shared the course with him. He followed the course to the letter. He went on to great success. I took the next step and went to a UPW (Unlimited Power Within) live seminar. It was held in Anaheim, Ca, just a short drive down the freeway from San Dimas. It was a three-day seminar and cost $600.00. Everyone I knew from the department laughed at me and thought paying $600.00 to go to a seminar was ridiculous. If I had not gone to that seminar, I would not have changed my thinking and philosophy in amazing ways. I would never have been promoted to sergeant, which meant $1,000.00 extra a month. And I retired at 70% of my pay, so that meant an extra $700 each month. That is just one aspect of my new way of thinking that put money in my pocket. So the value of that seminar to me is 1,000 times what I paid. There were 2,000 people at that seminar, which was a lot of people.

Fast forward 26 years later. My wife and I just went to a UPW seminar here in the Los Angeles Convention Center. There were 15,000 people. My wife had seen what going to the seminar had done for me and always wanted to go to a live event. I was ready to go again. We can always use a tune-up. She had done the 30-day tape program, and all the goals that she had written down came to be. So, she is a believer. It's great to be with someone likeminded. When I arrived at the seminar in 1993, all of a sudden I was with 2,000 likeminded people. This was great after being around so many naysayers at the department. I met a lady who owned a hair salon, and she brought her entire staff to the seminar. I met so many business-minded people, many of who had been to a seminar before.

The second day is the fire walk. I was prepared for the fire walk and had no fear or anxiety in doing it. Now, each day of the seminar goes from 8 am to about midnight or 1 am. Each day. So at around 10 pm on the second day, they march all 2,000 of us down to the parking lot, and the fire is roaring. The flames and extreme heat changed my state of mind. I started having some fear and anxiety. Your brain sees the fire, and your skin feels the heat. Your logical brain tells you that this is dangerous, don't touch. And parked in the driveway of the hotel near the parking lot is a firetruck and two ambulances. This told me that someone could get hurt. They take us back up to the conference room for two more hours of the seminar.

At about midnight, they take us back down, and by this time the flames were gone, and the red hot coals were spread out in about fifteen rows, fifteen feet long. And Tony is in the middle of the hot coals on a ladder, yelling, "More hot coals!" We were all in this together, so we all lined up and did our walks with no problem. It's not a trick, just a great metaphor for life. What else does your brain tell you, you can't do, but in fact you can do. Our brains are still running 2,000-year-old programs in an effort to protect us and keep us alive. Our environment has changed over 2,000 years, and sometimes we have to make conscious decisions based on what we believe now. It was great.

And on the last day, the speaker was Joseph Mcclendon. He spoke on health and nutrition. I remember he said he hadn't had a cold in 5 years. I thought, That is bullshit. And now having switched to a plant-based mostly vegan lifestyle, I can now say I haven't had a cold in 4 years. When Alba and I went to the seminar at the L.A. Convention Center, Joseph Mcclendon was still part of the seminar.

* * *

It was 1995, and I was working in a traffic car in San Dimas. I was set up working radar on the afternoon shift. I was on San Dimas Avenue when a BMW came into my radar at 65 mph in a 40 mph posted zone. I pulled out behind the BMW and activated my overhead emergency lights to conduct a traffic stop. The BMW did not stop, and the chase was on. I started broadcasting that I was in pursuit. I did see that the driver as he went by me looked like a youthful driver, so I put out over the radio that it was a possible stolen car.

We turned right on to Via Verde Avenue, now going westbound in the eastbound lanes, and the east and west lanes were divided by a median with big trees. This was not good. After about two hundred yards there was a break in the median, and the BMW jerked to the right now traveling west in the westbound lanes. Surprisingly the Watch Commander was still letting the pursuit continue. I had numerous backup units responding from all over to converge on my pursuit. We made a couple of quick turns, and the next thing you know we were in the parking lot of the Via Verde Country Club. We were screaming down the parking lot aisles, and people were throwing their clubs and jumping up on top of the back of their cars to avoid being hit. And then we were back on residential streets around the golf course. I had two other Sheriff cars join in the pursuit as an air unit came overhead and started calling the pursuit.

We came to a four-way stop, and the BMW suddenly stopped. I initiated a felony stop with my assisting units. The driver and lone occupant complied with my orders as I barked them over the loudspeaker. The driver was a 16 year old male Asian. He said he stole the car from his mother. The boy's parents came to the station to pick up their son. Until we called the house, they didn't know their car and son were missing. This kid was so polite, and he had no prior arrests. When I asked why he ran and didn't stop when I tried to pull him over, he said he had seen the O.J. pursuit on the news earlier in the day, and he thought it looked like fun. That's police work. Every day is different, and you see all sorts of crazy things.

I was now doing comedy again and working real estate out of a

Century 21 office in Pasadena. I had a friend working Temple Sheriff's Station which was about 10 miles east of San Dimas and a couple of miles southwest of Pasadena. He said he loved working at Temple Station. He made a case for me to transfer there.

He had worked with me at Lynwood Station. This sounded like the right move for me. I would be close to the Century 21 office in Pasadena, and I needed to be closer to Hollywood if I was going to continue my dreams in the entertainment industry. So I put my transfer in and in 1995 transferred to Temple Sheriff's Station Patrol.

TEMPLE STATION

I loved my time at Temple Station. I was there from the end of 1995 until the end of 1997. With my "can do" anything mindset, I was focusing on my acting and comedy career. I decided not to continue with my real estate. It was not feeding my soul. I produced a comedy show at the Roxy on Sunset that was a financial success. I produced a great tape out of it, but there was only so much I could do working my cop job full time and doing stand-up on my days off.

One pm shift I was behind a pickup truck and ran the plate. It returned with a felony warrant. I called for backup and initiated a traffic stop. The truck failed to stop and continued into a private driveway. As we approached to make the arrest, the driver got out and started walking away. I ordered him to stop, and he did. As I approached him, he knelt down and put his arms around the left front tire. My assisting unit and I approached, and each grabbed an arm. He let go of the tire, and the fight was on. He was mostly swinging his elbows in an effort to break free of our grasp. I lost my grip, and he broke free with his left arm. As my partner still had hold of his right arm, the suspect now tried to raise his left leg and kick me. I swing my baton to strike his kicking leg. I heard a loud "ouch!" Shit, I had struck my partner with my baton.

The suspect had now grabbed the top rim of the pickup truck bed. He wouldn't let go and tried to kick me on his left side as my partner was trying to pry his right arm off the truck. I thought I had a great idea. I reached around to the front of the suspect's face to pepper-spray him in the eyes. I let go with a two to three-second burst. I heard my partner yell, "You blinded me!" Shit, now I had pepper-sprayed my partner. I thought if I keep this up, my partner will be down, and I will be fighting this guy by myself.

The suspect finally submitted to arrest. Because we had used force on this guy, we had to transport him to the hospital to be cleared for booking. The field sergeant arrived at the hospital to get our statements and interview the suspect. I was videotaping the interview, and the suspect was telling the sergeant, "I'm fine, but I think that guy's partner got it worse than I did. I thought this guy might kill his partner and I would get blamed for it, so I gave up." Funny, but a little embarrassing. I don't think I landed a blow on this suspect, but I hit my partner with my baton and pepper-sprayed him in the face.

Mitch Hendrickson was a great friend of mine. We worked the South El Monte City area as sister cars. Mitch was a gentle giant of a man. He was a big guy, but I never saw him get angry. We played golf together. I talk a lot of shit on the golf course. I can make you angry. I was never able to rattle Mitch. We had many laughs at work and on the golf course. Mitch had two daughters and a lovely wife. And they seemed very happy.

A few months later, I was at our summer home in upstate New York, and I got a call from Mitch's wife. She said, "Cliff, I'm worried that Mitch is going to kill himself." I told her I would immediately call Mitch and our friend Javier. When I talked with Mitch on the phone, he said all was good, and when I told him about the call from his wife, he said it was ridiculous. I called Javier, who told me he got a similar call from Mitch's wife. He said he approached Mitch, who said, "Dude, stop, everything is good." A short time later, Mitch shot and killed himself. It was a strange thing. I was told a couple of days before he did this, he had tackled a guy who had threatened to jump off a bridge, saving his life.

I made it back in time for the funeral. The Undersheriff spoke and portrayed Mitch as a hero the best he could. It was a tough time with his two little daughters who I think were about 10 or 11. I will never understand it. I think about it from time to time, and when I talk to others about it, they say there is no way of knowing what someone is thinking in their mind. If they get it in their mind that this is what they're going to do, you can't stop them. I definitely believe in suicide prevention and looking for the signs. I always think maybe if I had been at work and could have been around Mitch as an influence, maybe it wouldn't have happened.

Deputy David March had a locker near mine. We didn't know each other very well, just a "how ya doing, hello goodbye" while changing between shifts in the locker room. I could tell by his conversations with others that he was a great guy with a positive attitude. Just how someone talks about how their day went, or how they interact with others tells you a great deal about their character. It must have been early 1998, and for some unknown reason, I found myself working the day shift. Maybe at that time I requested it. Most days I was working car 57, which was the Arcadia, Duarte, Monrovia county car. Car 57 is filled by two deputies on the pm and am shifts, but on day shift it is filled by one deputy. It was always quiet on day shift, and you didn't get too many calls. I would write a few tickets and make some car stops looking for arrests. I made numerous traffic stops on Live Oak Avenue east of Peck Road because it was nice and wide, and just had a couple of industry plants on it.

Just four years later, after I had transferred to West Hollywood, Deputy March was nearing the end of his time at Temple before transferring closer to his home in Santa Clarita. He was working 57-day shift and made a traffic stop on Live Oak Avenue east of Peck Road. He had no idea that the gang member driving the car had plotted to shoot a police officer on a traffic stop that day. The driver got out and walked toward Deputy March, meeting him between the two cars. The driver pulled out a gun and shot Dave, killing him and leaving him to lay in the street bleeding to death. The suspect was caught a couple of years later in Mexico, extradited, convicted, and sentenced to life in prison.

There is a memorial to Deputy March at the location where he was shot. I drove by and saw that it was the same area where I used to make traffic stops. Again I thought, But for the grace of God, go I. There is a memorial interchange sign at the 210 Freeway and the 605 Freeway. Another deputy that I knew personally. I pass the sign seeing his name, and it tugs at my heartstrings, also knowing that could have been me.

One night my girlfriend and future wife were at Universal Citywalk. We ran into an academy classmate of my girlfriend, and he was walking a foot beat at the Citywalk. I had never heard of this assignment before. I asked him, "You work here at the Citywalk and Universal Studios. You go to movie premiers on the job and work concerts at the Amphitheatre?" He said yea and told me about another 100 things that made this the assignment of a lifetime. Especially anyone interested in the entertainment industry, like me. I learned from my personal growth training how to get anything you want. Decide what you want, find out what you have to do to get it, and start doing those things.

I asked, "How do you get to work here."

He told me, "First you have to transfer to West Hollywood Station, and next you request to work the sub-station at the Citywalk."

I told him that was what I was going to do. A few short months later, my transfer came through for West Hollywood.

WEST HOLLYWOOD STATION

It was near the end of 1997 when I transferred into West Hollywood Station. This was an exciting place to work. West Hollywood was a contract city. Instead of having their own police force, they contracted with the Sheriff's Department. This was a 10 million dollar contract. West Hollywood was home to stars, hookers, the sunset strip, and the Russian mob. The station was also responsible for patrol duties at Universal Studios and the Citywalk which were on county property. Actually, part of the Citywalk is in the City of L.A., so many times we had turf arguments as to who was responsible for certain crimes and reports.

I had to keep in mind that my main goal was to get to the Universal Sub-station because I was having a ball at the city. Remember when I was patrolling the lonely roads of Livingston County NY, it was an ad in Police Product News magazine, "Ride the strip, we pay the gas" with a Sheriff's car driving down the strip that prompted me to apply to the Sheriff's Department. Now here I was, driving a Sheriff's car down the sunset strip. Dream fulfilled. LAPD Hollywood Division has the shitty part of Hollywood, and we had the strip. Driving down the strip was like driving in a movie. I was driving and talking to myself, and there was the Comedy Store, the Roxbury, The Whiskey A-Go-Go, The Viper Room, the Roxy and then the strip ends. You know the strip ends traveling west because you see that Welcome to Beverly Hills sign.

I'm driving through Beverly Hills checking out all the spots I saw in the movie Beverly Hills Cop. I was on the job getting paid and taking myself on my own celebrity tour. There was always a nice surprise as I drove around the city discovering new landmarks. Right near the station was the Troubadour, where Lenny Bruce was arrested in the 1960s. And the city loved the Sheriff's Department. You could pull up in an alley behind a fancy restaurant. The staff would come out and drape a white tablecloth across your hood and lay all the place settings out and serve you lobster on the hood. Seems like somebody always paid for your meal before you could. This wasn't all the time, or everywhere. But if you developed the right relationships, life at West Hollywood was amazing.

The city demographics were predominantly gay. There is a line of gay night clubs on Santa Monica Blvd. The hookers on Santa Monica Blvd. were male and don't come out until a certain hour. Some of the hookers on Santa Monica Blvd. were transgender, or he/shes. Driving down the street late at night, if you didn't know the area, you wouldn't know these hookers were male. The female hookers worked on Sunset Blvd.

I was really enjoying my time at the city, and then one day I was called into the Scheduling Deputy's office. He started apologizing to me, saying there was nothing he could do because I was the last person to transfer in, he had to send me up to work the Citywalk sub-station. I didn't tell him that's why I came to the station in the first place. I think I did pretty good hiding my excitement. I told him that I was there to serve the station and wherever he needed me to go, I was there to help. He was so thankful. He told me that he would never forget that I went without complaint. I rode that goodwill for about five years. If I needed a day off or vacation time, he always approved it. So off to Universal I went for the next five years.

UNIVERSAL

Universal was a different world. It was about five or six miles from the home station. We had a station right at the Citywalk on the second floor that we shared with the uniformed security officers. Universal is a big property. We had patrol responsibilities for the back lot where all the sound stages were and where they gave the studio tour, also for the theme park and the Universal Amphitheater. We also covered the Citywalk and the surrounding parking structures. Our patrol shifts started at 6 am and ended around two or three in the morning, depending on the activity. So for about two to three hours, police calls would have to be handled by the West Hollywood city cars. There is a bank that faces the street on Lankershim but is actually on Universal property. So we also had that.

One morning many years before I got there, the bank had been robbed at gunpoint. It was early in the morning sometime around 7 am. The bank was not open yet; employees were inside and tied up. A lot of money was taken. After the robbery, the department promised Universal to always have deputies on duty at six am. So day shift at Universal was a good gig. You started at 6 am, and the theme park, stores, and restaurants didn't open until 10 am. By the time anything was really happening, your shift was half over. I'd like to say it was all fun and games, and it was. But there were some nights all went bad. During the day and up until about nine at night, the clientele were mostly families walking around and leaving the theme park.

After nine pm on the weekends, there was a heavy gang presence. There was some type of understanding between the gangs that Universal was neutral territory. Either because of choice or necessity based on the heavy police presence. But every so often, someone would throw a gang sign or give a wrong look to the wrong person, and the fight would be on. On rare occasion, the shooting would be on. But these incidents reinforced the need for our presence. Part of our job was to be seen, to give patrons a feeling of security with our presence, and put the crooks on notice. This was no place for them to be capering.

For the most part, things went smoothly. If they went too smoothly for too long, the Universal Executives would be walking around seeing us standing around having coffee and laughing. In their minds they are thinking, Are we paying these guys for this? Do we need armed, uniformed deputy sheriff's around here? And then someone would get beat up, shot or robbed, and that was the reminder. We need the police close by.

The Universal Amphitheater was just a hundred yards behind the sub-station. Depending on the concert and the type of clientele it attracted, they would hire deputies for overtime. Sometimes it was easy money, and sometimes it was a crazy time. This was a great venue to have as our patrol responsibility. It was a lot of extra overtime money, and it was fun. And we had a great relationship with the management of the venue. For any event, we had first access to purchase house seats at regular prices. House seats were orchestra seats and anywhere in the first ten rows.

Chris Rock did a concert there, and I signed up to work overtime for the event. I watched the whole concert standing in the back. After the show, I went back to the green room and met Chris Rock, Jerry Seinfeld, Madonna, and Carl Reiner. I had recently met Jerry Seinfeld on the set of his show. I was taking acting lessons with Judy Kerr, who was the dialogue coach on the show. She arranged for me to do extra work on the show. I was a patron in the coffee shop. One show that I worked as an extra the guest star was James Spader. The day before doing the extra work, I had actually seen Jerry driving one of his Porsche's down Sunset at a good clip. I didn't stop him. While waiting for the scene to shoot, I told Judy to tell Jerry that I saw him speeding on Sunset and didn't stop him because I was going to be on the show. He laughed and came up and introduced himself to me. Alba (my wife) and I did extra work together on the very last show of Seinfeld.

Alba transferred to West Hollywood Station in 1998. She was having a great time working the city, and I was having a great time up at Universal. She met a contact at the Argyle Hotel in West Hollywood. Every Monday night, Jeff Goldbloom played piano in the lounge of the hotel. We went down a couple of times to hear him play. Not too many people knew at the time that he was a world-class jazz pianist. When he played in the Argyle Lounge, it was not to any fanfare. There maybe was fifty to one hundred people in the lounge enjoying his music. Now in 2019, he's releasing an album.

The manager of the Argyle took Alba and me around the hotel and gave us some of the history. Wow, it was a pretty amazing tour. He took us to the penthouse suite, which had a balcony that went around the top of the hotel. The manager told us that John Wayne used to stay there, and he always had a cow on the balcony because he wanted fresh milk daily. He took us into another room and showed us a burn mark in the rug. He said it was from a cigar Oliver Stone dropped when he fell asleep smoking. Not sure if these stories were true, but fascinating none the less.

Things were going great at the department and in my comedy and acting career. Having been to Tony Robbins and having an unlimited mindset, I set out on another lifelong dream. I had success doing my show at the Roxy on Sunset, so that inspired me to the next level. Richard Pryor released a comedy DVD called Live on The Sunset Strip. I loved the look of the stage and venue on the DVD. I checked the credits and saw that it had been filmed at the Hollywood Palladium. Before leaving NY in 1983, I had put in my subconscious mind that I wanted to do a comedy special at the Hollywood Palladium.

It was now 1998, and I made an appointment with the owner of the Palladium. He turned out to be one of 12 owners. But he was the man handling the office and daily function of the Palladium. He was a reserve officer with the Culver City Police department, so we hit it off right away. He told me I could rent the Palladium during the week for $5500.00. But that would just be what they call four walls. I would have to provide the spotlights and sound. I had some money from the Roxy show, tax returns, and some savings. I gave him a check and signed a contract.

I had a few months before the show, giving me time to sell tickets and fill the Palladium. It holds almost 3,000 people. But the bottom floor can look full with 1,000. I even went to a publicist. She said, "I'm not gonna take your money; you're not a name; you will never fill the Palladium." She meant well, but I thought, Watch me, lady. I didn't know how; I just knew it was gonna happen.

A few weeks after signing the contract, the owner of the Palladium called me and said, "Paramount Studios just called me. They're doing the re-release of Grease, and they want the Palladium on your date. I told them I already had a contract with you, and they offered $5500.00 for you to change your date."

I don't know why I told him this, it just flew out of my mouth. "I have already spent money promoting and selling tickets, it will cost them $9,000.00 for me to change the date."

The owner said he was kind of the whore in this deal. I told him if the studio paid the $9,000, I would have a brokerage fee for him. He said, "I know what to do." Now I talked to all my acting friends in the business, and they all asked what was wrong with me. Why didn't I take the $5500.00, where did I get the $9,000 figure from? I didn't know, and I hadn't spent any money yet, so the $5500.00 would have been free money.

The Palladium owner called me back and said, "They're gonna pay you the $9,000.00, write up a billing voucher to Paramount for the amount." I met him for lunch later in the week, and I pushed an envelope with $500.00 cash in it across the table to him. He said, "Did the studios pay you yet?" When I told him no, he said, "I don't trust them. When they pay you, then I'll take your envelope." Wow, what a standup guy. It did take a while and several phone calls to get them to send the check finally. But they did, and I met with the owner, and he got his envelope. Now I made $9,000, and I hadn't opened the doors yet.

I had a good friend Mike Marino opening for me. And I had two other lady comedians in the show. Margaret Cho was our MC. I don't even know how that happened. Mike was a very successful actor, but his true love was standup comedy. Now he is a major headliner all over the country. He has numerous TV and film credits, and when I'm lucky, he hires me to open for him. We went on to do more than 100 shows together. Now that we had this money, Mike and I put a full-page and a half-page in Daily Variety. Mike at the time was teaching comedy traffic school and had met some members of the Hells Angels Motorcycle gang through traffic school. We sold some tickets, and then decided to comp the rest of the tickets to fill the place and get a good tape out of it. Between my Sheriff's Department friends and Mike's Hells Angels, we had over 1,000 fill the bottom floor. I was glad that the publicist came to the show. I told her on the way out, "Told you I would fill it."

She said, "You did it." We had people from The Tonight Show and several film studios respond to be on our VIP guest list. The show went on without a hitch. My mom, dad, and cousin flew out from NY to see the show. I did my show at the Hollywood Palladium. Another dream fulfilled.

The next year in 1999, the Sheriff's Aide called me. He said, "Cliff, the Sheriff would like you to do a comedy show fundraiser to help raise money for a float he is putting in the Rose Parade." I told him I was in. We did it at the Country Star Restaurant on the Citywalk. This time I opened for Mike Marino. He was already on his way as a major headliner one year after our Palladium show. It was a great success, and the Sheriff was very happy. Amazing what a change in attitude and philosophy can do. From working at San Dimas Station and the lieutenant telling my friends to stay away from me or it would hurt their career. And now the Sheriff was calling me to do a fundraiser for his float.

I was working the dayshift, and they were preparing for the Country Music Awards at the Amphitheater. I walked down and sat in the balcony to watch the rehearsal for that night's show. This was very exciting. I was walking back to the sub-station on the service road between the Citywalk and theme park, and these two big white dudes with long black coats and cowboy hats were walking toward me. They asked me how to get to the Amphitheater. I told them I would walk them down there. They said, "We are Montgomery Gentry." I think it was their first year at the CMA's. The lead deputy at Universal also ran a security company that handled after parties from the CMA's. That night he was working one at the nearby Universal Hilton, and he invited Alba and me to come to the party. Some of the acts would take to a makeshift stage and sing a few of their songs. Montgomery Gentry got up and sang a few songs, laughing and drinking a couple of beers. It was a fun night.

My memory of meeting them flooded back into my brain when I was watching the CMA Wwards in 2017. All of a sudden a bunch of well-known country artists were singing on stage with Eddie Montgomery. They were showing a picture of Troy Gentry and panning to a lady and child in the front row of the audience. I didn't know that Troy Gentry had been killed in a helicopter crash. Two months earlier Montgomery Gentry was about to start a concert at a resort in New Jersey. Troy Gentry opted to take a pre-show helicopter ride that was offered to them by the resort. The helicopter crashed, killing the pilot instantly. Troy Gentry survived to the hospital, later dying of his injuries at age fifty.

Growing up, I listened to all the country stars of the time because my mom constantly played the records in the house. I remember hearing "Rose Garden" by Lynne Anderson a few hundred times. That song came out in 1970. Twenty-eight years later in 1998, I was working the foot beat at the Citywalk. Who came out of the Amphitheatre after the Country Music Awards, needing to be walked to her limousine? Lynne Anderson. I walked her to her Limo, and we had a little chat on our walk. What a nice lady.

One year they held the MTV awards at the Amphitheater, and the after-party was the entire theme park. MTV had rented out the entire theme park at Universal Studios. They agreed through an arrangement with the studios to hire 25-30 Sheriff personnel, but none in uniform. So there were 25 or so of us at the rank of deputy working in plainclothes mingling in the MTV Awards after-party with nine open bars.

I remember walking the Citywalk with my partner Rick, and Channel 9 was doing some promo for their spot on the news covering the MTV Awards. We had a long talk with the reporters and crew. They did a spot with us on the news. We told them we would be changing out of our uniforms to work inside the MTV after-party. They said, "We want to go to the after-party."

Rick said, "Come with us. We will walk you into the party." As we walked with them, I told the producer about my comedy life, and she said maybe they would do a segment profiling my work at Universal and my work as a comedian. We exchanged numbers, and I never expected to hear from her. I thought it was just friendly banter as we walked them into the party. Sure enough, a few weeks later they sent a film crew out to film Rick and I walking our beat. Then a week or so later they filmed me doing a set at the world-famous Comedy Store on the strip. They put together a nice piece which aired on L.A.'s Channel 9, and it's still on YouTube. From a U-turn on Route 390 in upstate New York to performing at the world-famous Comedy Store on the Sunset Strip and profiled on the Los Angeles News. Follow your dreams. They will come true.

Every weekend we did a curfew sweep at 10 pm. There was a county ordinance curfew that the studios made use of to keep unaccompanied minors off the Citywalk after 10 pm. It also helped in keeping the gang element away too. We would start at one end of the walk. At the front of the loosely formed skirmish line would be the Universal uniformed security officers. There would be about ten of them. With them were the Universal nonuniform security officers who were mostly off duty LAPD officers, and there were about six of them. There might be one or two county probation officers also. Then bringing up the rear were us, usually a sergeant and about six deputies. Security would make the initial contact to youthful-looking patrons. If they had no I.D. or were unaccompanied minors, they would call one of us up. Depending on the circumstance, we would escort them up to the station for a ticket and a call to their parents or guardian to come pick them up.

Sounds simple enough, but most of the time it never went that smooth. Someone would challenge the security officer and maybe even assault them. By the time we jump in, the fight could be on. And after the fray was over and people were in handcuffs headed to jail, many times they would be surprised they were actually being charged with battery on a peace officer. People have the image of the police as coming to a scene and getting out of a marked police car. So many times, seeing us in uniform on a foot beat would not click that we were the actual police. They would sometimes stupidly assume we were security guards.

We would repeat this curfew sweep again around midnight. And then after the clubs closed at 2 am, we would have to clear the Citywalk of people who would gather and refuse to leave. There was a lot of pepper-spray used, and a lot of force on occasion.

My sub-station lieutenant was a great guy. He was a super cop and war veteran. He was always looking for ways to help me make connections in the entertainment industry. In 1998 they had the premiere and after-party for the movie Patch Adams, starring Robin Williams. The lieutenant convinced the studios that there had been rumors of terrorist threats against Hollywood, which was true. But he convinced them they should have a couple of undercover deputies in the after-party just in case. The lieutenant wanted me to meet Robin Williams. I did meet Robin Williams for a hot second in the after-party, but his attention was in demand. After the party, my lieutenant arranged for me to take Robin Williams's publicist to his car. I don't know what that connection would garner, and it didn't any. But the lieutenant was always looking out for my cop and comedy career.

September 11, 2001. Everyone remembers where they were on that morning. I was on the way to Universal sub-station for the start of my day shift. It was around 5:30 am, and I was on the freeway when the first plane hit. I was at the sub-station starting my shift when the second plane hit. I think this became the only time in history that Universal closed the CityWalk and theme park. I have a video of the lieutenant and me driving a Sheriff's car down Citywalk, and it looked like a ghost town.

On the Citywalk, which was full of tourists from all over the world, it was mostly positive and friendly interactions with us. People always wanted their picture taken with us, and we obliged. It was a great way to interact with people that weren't in crisis. Usually, in patrol, most of our contact was with victims of crimes, tragedy, or

133

criminals. After 9/11 there was a wave across the whole country of people showing support for police, firefighters and all first responders.

One night I was walking with my partner in the hallway of the Amphitheater. We were there to work at some country concert. We never worked inside the theatre. They had staff security for that. And any unruly or fighting patrons would be brought out to us for escort off the property or arrest. We would walk inside the building but outside the theatre proper, or inside the house as they say. We were contacted by a lone senior lady. She was probably in her 80's, so I think it's ok to say she was a senior. She needed help back to her seat to join the rest of her party. She had a cane and was not moving well. I recognized that we were right in front of the section where her seat was. Instead of calling one of the ushers, I decided to walk her to her seat because I knew it was just a few rows inside the doors. It was close enough to showtime that the place was nearly full but far enough ahead that all the house lights were up. As she sat down in her aisle seat, I just held her arm and guided her into her seat. As I turned to walk away, the entire crowd broke out into applause. After 9/11, people just wanted to show their support. Seeing a uniformed deputy sheriff help a lady to her seat, they applauded, saying thank you and we support you.

This was an amazing time. It only lasted a year or two. Especially in California, people were back to cop-hating and bashing in short order. I know not everybody, but a great majority of California liberals especially just tolerate the police but don't really support them. They believe the police are a necessary evil.

My wonderful lieutenant had arranged for Alba and me to attend some movie premiere. I can't remember which one now. And after the movie, Alba and I were sitting at a table having our meal and cocktail. It was just Alba and me, and one other guy. Then a lady came and sat down next to the guy. They were really nice. She introduced us to the guy. "This is my husband Brad Paisley. He's a singer." We were sitting with country superstar Brad Paisley before he was a country superstar. Sometimes you meet people before they really make it, and you see how nice and humble they are. And then they make it big, and you're happy for those people.

* * *

One night after the Country Music Awards, we were keeping the crowd away from Faith Hill who was doing an Entertainment Tonight interview. The crowd was pushing in. We were about two feet away from Faith Hill. She looks beautiful on TV, and in person even more beautiful. She was stunning. I look to my left, and I see a guy standing in front of Faith. He is being pushed and shoved pretty good, and I recognize him. It was Faith's husband, Tim McGraw. You wouldn't recognize him at the time without his cowboy hat on. He looks totally different. This was before he had done many movies. Now he would be recognized right away. I thought that must have been humbling for him. Everyone was trying to push past him to get a look at his wife, and nobody even saw him. He didn't look shaken at all.

The film producer Robert Zemeckus had a bungalow office on the lower lot of Universal Studios. He made a police report when he discovered that his bungalow had been broken into. Stolen were his People's Choice Award, a Forest Gump hat signed by Tom Hanks, and a laptop computer with the personal information of his Hollywood elite friends. It was a few days later when a transient was arrested on the backlot who had been living under the old west movie set facade. He was arrested for trespassing, but he had no stolen items on him.

One night my super cop lieutenant came into the sub-station on a mission. He said he couldn't believe nobody had solved this case yet. He looked at me and said, "Cliff, you should have solved this. If you had solved the case and returned his stolen items, Robert Zemeckus would have you in every movie he makes." He said it was obvious that the transient who was arrested on the backlot was behind the burglary and theft from Zemeckus' bungalow. Then he sent a Sheriff's car from the West Hollywood Station to bring the transient back up to the sub-station. The suspect was a male from Mexico and spoke no English. The lieutenant said, "The detectives have had this case for over a week, and they haven't solved this yet. I'm going to do it tonight." He had a trainee translate for him.

I don't know what he said to this suspect, but the suspect admitted to the break-in and stealing from the bungalow on the lower lot. Through a deputy translating the statements of the suspect, he said he knew where the stolen Forest Gump hat was and the People's Choice Award. He agreed to direct us to the location of the stolen items.

The lieutenant pointed to me and said, "Get two more marked units, and let's go get the stolen property back."

I got a couple marked units to accompany me as we followed the lieutenant in his unmarked car. He had the deputy who was translating and the suspect in his car. We caravanned to the washroom of an apartment complex in North Hollywood. We got out of our cars, and the lieutenant said, "He says the hat is in a plastic bag behind a washing machine." The lieutenant walked into the small laundry room, reached behind the washer and pulled out a green plastic garbage bag. Sure enough, in the bag was a Forest Gump hat signed by Tom Hanks. We got back in our cars, and over the radio, the lieutenant said we were headed for downtown L.A.

We arrived at the "Cliftons Cafe," a famous deli in downtown Los Angeles. Now it was about 11 pm, and everything was closed. We got out of our cars, and the suspect was out too. The suspect was peering through a small hole in a closed overhead metal door to a gold trading business. He said this was the place where the People's Choice Award was sold and the laptop computer. The lieutenant had the desk somehow contact the owner who came down and opened up his shop, and unbelievably the People's Choice Award and laptop were there. Case solved.

They had the premiere party for American Pie 2 at the Hard Rock Cafe on the CityWalk. The Lieutenant, myself, and a group of deputies were assigned to the detail. We had some problems with aggressive paparazzi. Wow, they can really get out of hand when trying to get a picture of celebrities. These pictures are big business, and when a celebrity is not cooperative in giving them a shot at a great picture, they can get very nasty. Everything went pretty smoothly, and we had no major incidents during the party. It was pretty much breaking up when the lieutenant told me he was leaving, and that I could release the deputies on the detail whenever I thought it looks good. A short time later, when it looked like most everyone had left the Hard Rock, I released the deputies.

Myself and one other deputy were left on the CityWalk. We got a call of a disturbance from the studio security. There was a disturbance by the valet stand near the Hard Rock. I headed in that direction as the only deputy from the detail left at the Citywalk. There was a ton of security officers around, those normally assigned to the Citywalk and those who were working the premier party provided by the studio. When I got to the valet area, several overly aggressive paparazzi were trying to push their way toward celebrities who were waiting for their cars at the valet stand. They had no respect for the space that the security officers were trying to maintain between themselves and the celebrities. I arrived in time to see one cameraman push a security officer out of his way as he took a picture. After taking his picture, he grabbed another security officer by the shirt who was trying to move him back behind some ropes designated to keep the crowd back from the valet area.

Because of the crowd, I could not get to the camera guy who had already committed battery on two security officers. When I saw him draw an arm back to hit a security officer, I deployed a stream of pepper-spray perfectly over the shoulder of actor Bill Paxton to the eyes of our cameraman. This was a distance of about fifteen feet. I was just glad that I hadn't inadvertently sprayed Bill Paxton. That definitely would have ended up as a national news event. My camera guy was affected immediately by the pepper-spray and went down to the ground rubbing his eyes with his free hand. I quickly got to him and arrested him for battery without further incident. When I got him back to the sub-station, I found out that he was a freelance cameraman and not affiliated with any major publication.

I called my lieutenant on the phone, and he started yelling, "This could be a major national story by tomorrow morning. I'm on the way down there." He came down, but quickly realized himself that the guy we arrested was a goofball with no national ties with any major publication. He was an independent who got pictures of celebrities and entertainment events and sold them to the news or major entertainment publications. Sometimes we would hold our breath in these kinds of deals to see if it makes the national news. You never know who got pictures or video and of what. A video of me pepper-spraying a cameraman over the shoulder of Bill Paxton might have ended up on TMZ or wherever. The next thing you know, the Sheriff himself will want to know what went on. There were no incidents too small not to be concerned might blow up into something.

I don't remember the year, but the female wrestler Chyna had an event scheduled at Universal Citywalk. She was signing pictures or a book, I can't remember exactly. But we had a large crowd gathered waiting for her to arrive. She was really late, and the crowd was getting bigger and more upset that she wasn't there yet. A supervisor who was in charge of the event found out that she was going to be coming from an appearance at The Tonight Show. The supervisor sent a deputy down to The Tonight Show to escort her back to the Citywalk right after she got off stage with Jay Leno. The deputy actually went into the studio and was waiting offstage for Chyna to come off the couch. The deputy said he told her and her driver, "You have to get to Universal right now, and I'm going to escort you straight there." The deputy got her up to the signing right away without incident. But these are the kinds of crazy things that happened on a nightly basis. Chyna was very nice and took pictures with all the deputies. She died in 2016 from a combination of drugs and alcohol.

One night I'm at the back gate of the Citywalk talking with the security officer. Who drives up for her performance for the night but Stevie Nicks. I can't remember if it was a solo performance or if she was performing as the lead singer of Fleetwood Mac. It was surprising that some celebrities arrive at events in a limousine and some who live in the area just drive their own car. Stevie Nicks was driving to her concert in her own car, alone. She got to the gate and asked how to get to the Amphitheatre for her performance. I told her I would escort her down to the backstage entrance.

I was about sixteen years old, and my mom and dad had taken me to the movies in Henrietta, NY just outside of Rochester. My dad pointed to a guy in the lobby getting popcorn and said, "That's Bob Forster, a famous actor." I didn't think that much of it at the time. As he became more and more famous for roles in Police Story and then Jackie Brown, I started following his career. His hometown was Rochester, NY It might have been for the movie Jackie Brown, but either way, I'm on my foot beat walking the CityWalk and who comes walking from the parking lot but Robert Forster. He parked his car in the public parking lot to attend a movie premiere at the Universal Amphitheater. I walked him to the theatre and talked with him for a minute. I told him about the time my dad pointed him out at the theatre in Rochester. I recently saw him on a plane from L.A. to NY. Some of my friends and I were on our way to our annual pilgrimage to NY during the Christmas season. My friend sat right next to Robert for the whole trip. I said hi to him and reminded him how we first met, and he asked if I ever got back to Rochester. I asked him the same, and he said he gets back there a couple of times a year.

Meeting Will Smith was a great pleasure. He is a real nice, humble man. We had a special request to meet him at the back of the movie theaters at the CityWalk. Myself and another deputy with some security officers met him at the back door. He had on a baseball cap and a big coat. He explained that he liked to slip in the back of the theatre to see the reaction of the crowd as they watch the movie. We escorted him to the proper theatre, but not really escorting so that anyone would know that he was anybody. And when he pulled that ball cap down over his eyes, you wouldn't know it was anyone well-known. When the movie was over, he slipped out the back door to an awaiting car, and he was gone.

Michael Jackson did the same thing. I can't remember what movie it was, but he was not so inconspicuous. He had worn some kind of face mask and had quite an entourage. We waited for the movie to start, and he was escorted up to a balcony section that was closed off to the public so he could see the crowd watching the movie below, but no one knew he was there.

On the top floor of the Citywalk were several clubs and restaurants, one of which was B.B. King's. It was a great Jazz Club that always had famous Jazz musicians stopping by or performing as part of the schedule. It was a nice place with a great stage. Once a year, BB

King would show up, and it was a big deal. I don't know how many clubs he had. If I remember right, they said he tried to visit them all once a year. I know the employees always looked forward to him coming. He would tip each of the staff $100 on his visit. I never met him personally, but I know everyone loved him, and everyone who had met him said he was the nicest man.

The craziest thing Universal did was have Halloween Horror Nights. This lasted about ten days or so before Halloween. It was every night before Halloween inside the theme park. They had guys dressed up with chainsaw motors. Guys would jump out from behind trees with these damn chain saws scaring the hell out of people. Sometimes they did too good a job. People would get startled, and they would punch the theme park employee, and then we would have people being arrested. A lot of people got drunk before or while they were attending the Horror Nights, which led to more trouble. For the ten days or so they put this on, they had to hire about twenty deputies on overtime each night. I think they paid in the neighborhood of $30,000 in overtime for the week. But they packed them in for Horror Nights. There was so much overtime that we couldn't supply enough personnel. So we hired from outside stations. And they hired motor officers from all over the county. The rest of the county thought it was great to work overtime at Universal. But for those of us that worked the unit as a regular, the Horror Nights were a pain in the neck. Maybe that was more my take on it. The overtime was amazing. You could work 10 or 12 hours of overtime each of the Horror Nights, that you weren't working your regular shift. And if you worked the day shift, you could work more of it.

New Year's eve was another crazy time at the CityWalk. It wasn't New York Times Square, but they did their best to create the same type of atmosphere. Even now when they switch coverage from NY to L.A. they will cut to coverage at the Citywalk. Everyone is packed in, and there is no moving through that crowd. This is another night where they hire overtime deputies from all over the county. There will be SWAT teams, K9 teams, special enforcement teams, and regular deputies stationed all over Universal. A couple of times, my wife and I were able to work the overtime on New Year's eve together. Many of the posts are on the top floor or rooftop looking down on the action because there is no way you can move around.

There were never any major problems during the New Year's Eve celebrations. After 2 am and the bars closed, we would have the usual fights and arrests we had every weekend. But during these special events, we always had plenty of coverage with the overtime deputies. The problems happened when it was not a special event, and nothing had been scheduled. And then all of a sudden we would find out there was an event scheduled on the Citywalk or at the Amphitheater, and no one on the Sheriff's department side knew anything about it. Usually, we had weeks if not months prior notice to special events where they expected a large crowd. Usually, there would be several meetings determining what resources were needed regarding public safety.

Every year Shaq O'Neil had an event on the Citywalk. It was a thrill to meet him and actually talk to him. When I met Shaq he was already a reserve officer. Shaq loved the police and always had time to talk and spend time with officers. After one of Shaq's annual basketball events, three other deputies and I walked him to his car in the parking garage at Universal. Before he left the Citywalk at his prompting, we took a bunch of pictures. He really is a nice man. Sometimes you never know. I had always liked Arnold Schwarzenegger and not really cared for Lou Ferrigno. We had to provide security for Arnold at some event on the Citywalk. He was the most unfriendly, rude person you would ever want to meet. Maybe he had a bad day. But he definitely showed no signs of being a supporter of the police. On the other hand, Lou Ferrigno was the most humble, kind person you would ever meet. And he was interested in what you had to say. His dad had been with the NYPD, and his support for law enforcement was obvious.

Joseph Nasser, a producer friend of mine, was a reserve for the department along with Lou Ferrigno. I was sent to Mr. Nasser's house to assist with a promotional video they were making for the reserve recruitment unit. After filming, Mr. Nasser provided lunch for me, Lou and Joe's kids. We had a great time, and I had the best time talking with Lou. So many years after his competitive bodybuilding days, and he is still strict with his diet. He wanted to know exactly what he was eating at lunch. It was all plant-based as I think back on it. Lou was still in fantastic shape.

My two stints at Universal, first as a deputy then as a sergeant, I have to say were the best years I had on the Sheriff's department. Having spent so many years in patrol and loving patrol, it was a nice change to still be in a patrol assignment, but now one that was almost entirely a foot beat. And not any foot beat, but at one of the premier entertainment centers of the country. Walking and talking with all the restaurant, store, and theme park employees was a pleasure. I met many that became close friends even to this day. It was fun taking pictures with and talking to tourists from all over the world. Watching the street entertainers and enjoying the nightlife while getting paid was a great gig. One minute you're walking the Citywalk. The next your part of a detail along with the state department guarding Benjamin Netanyahu, as he takes a private tour of the backlot. That was an interesting day. They didn't close down the backlot tours. But Netanyahu got a private tour car to take him and his family on the backlot tour. We had a Sheriff's car following. On the tram with Netanyahu were armed members of the state department and Netenyahu's own security detail who were packing submachine guns. Fun times, I have many fond memories of my patrol days at Universal.

SERGEANTS EXAM

I had never wanted to promote to sergeant; in fact, I probably was a sergeant's nightmare at times. My good friend and sergeant at Universal told me that he wanted me to promote, so I would have to supervise someone like myself. Top step sergeant's pay is $1,000 more a month than top step deputy's pay. I figured if I retired at 75% of my pay, my sergeant's portion of retirement alone would be $750 every month. So, that was my motive for wanting to promote the last couple of years of my career. A group of us started studying for the Sergeant's Exam.

In the early days of the department, you would take the Sergeant's Exam, and after the written, oral and some other factors you would be listed as eligible for promotion on a numerical list. If you were number 75 you would be promoted after 74, and so on. Then there was a female on the Sergeant's List that powers that be didn't want to be promoted. When her number was coming up, they would end the list and announce a new test. She went to court, and the court determined that the department had in fact discriminated against the female applicant based on her sex. The court invoked something called injunctive relief. The applicant had to be promoted, and the department would have to revamp the promotion process with court oversight.

Before they started giving the exam again, the court approved the banding process. Whereby the eligible candidates for promotion would be grouped into bands, everyone in band one would have to be promoted before anyone in band two could be promoted. In my opinion, this allowed for more discrimination than the old system. The department had options in their discriminatory ambitions. They could have a very small band one, and then a huge band two or three. When they promote from a band, the only requirement is to promote from the band until that band is exhausted, but you can pick anyone you want from the band. If you have a band of 200 and you get 40 of your buddies in the band, you can just promote your buddies and nobody else. Now, there was a based on sex remedy. The court did order that a certain percentage of promotions had to be female. So in that regard, it prevented the department from not promoting females. But they could make sure they got their females in the band, which would allow them to discriminate against individual females. The department was under the court consent decree for over 20 years, so I have to lay some of this groundwork as I talk about promoting to sergeant.

I took the Sergeant's Exam and did pretty good. As in the example I gave earlier, the department created a small band one of about 20 candidates and then there was a large band two and three. I was in band two along with another 100 or so candidates. But the rumor was that all of band two would get promoted. Sometimes these lists would last two years, so the numbers could move quickly. Remember, we have about 10,0000 sworn positions.

My new-found positive attitude and influence had me developing some powerful relationships within the department. And working at the Universal Sub-Station allowed me the opportunity to help quite a few power players out when it came to their entertainment appetites. Several times a week executives at some level would call and want some assistance with either discounts, or free admission into the Universal Theme Park. Many times I was allotted VIP complimentary passes into the park, and I would use these when certain Commanders or other similar level executives wanted to bring their family into the park. The department would promote groups of sergeants at a time— ten here, fifteen there. So after a few lists for promotion to sergeant came out and I wasn't on the list, I was a little peeved.

Prone as I was never to follow the chain of command and go over the heads of my direct supervisors, I went down to the Sheriff's headquarters to meet with assistant Sheriff Stonich. While I was waiting outside his office, a commander came by and said, "Cliff, are you here to get an award or something?"

I told him, "No, I'm here to see the assistant Sheriff about this promotion process." He happened to be my Commander for region two which covered West Hollywood Station and the Universal Sub-station. I had arranged for this Commander and many of his family to gain entry into Universal and special events on numerous occasions.

So I was happy that he came by and saw me. I wanted to send a message: I've done quite a bit for you. Leave me behind, and I will spill the beans on some of your activities.

He did make some valid points. He asked me, "Cliff, have you gone to the Deputy Leadership Institute?" I told him no, and he asked me, "Have you put in for an operations unit?" I told him that I hadn't. I thanked him for his advice and direction, and that I would do those things. I relayed my conversation to the Assistant Sheriff and just asked if he saw my name on a specialized unit list, to please consider me.

I applied to attend the Deputy Leadership Institute (DLI), which was a one or two week deal. I was chosen to go and really loved it. It was all about leadership skills, positivity, and motivation. Many of the books they had at the program were books I had read on my own. Some of these books were books I was exposed to during my real estate seminars and training. Some were books that had been suggested reading by Tony Robbins. And many were new. We would read these books on our own, and then discuss them during the class. The class was conducted in a facilitation style. We had group discussions led by a facilitator, and we would have break out groups. We would come up with discussion points, write them on a flip chart, and bring our findings back to the big group. Each person got the chance in their group to be the spokesperson. I learned a lot about facilitation concepts just by attending. I was in DLI class 3, so this was a relatively new concept of training adopted by the department.

We watched many movies. Some war pictures like 12 O'clock High were perfect for a leadership discussion. Since I was already into personal development, I was overjoyed to be getting paid to learn more skills which would help me grow as a person on and off duty. After the training, I attended the facilitator training so I could be a DLI facilitator. Many of the DLI facilitators were sergeants and lieutenants. So joining this group was another avenue to develop relationships with people who could do things for me.

I found it funny that I had put in for several specialized unit jobs and never was chosen. All of a sudden, I got a call asking if I wanted to go to the Equity Training Unit. I had applied to the same unit for a different position, so I had interviewed there but was not chosen for that particular position. The position they picked me for was to facilitate the court imposed sexual harassment training which came out of the consent decree as one of the results of the Sergeant's Exam lawsuit.

For over a year, the training of department executives had been conducted by professional consultants from the firm "Price Waterhouse Coopers." Part of the consent decree agreement would be for the consulting group to develop and implement a train the trainers' curriculum for the sexual harassment policy. My experience attending and becoming a facilitator for the Deputy Leadership Institute helped me get the job at the Equity Training Unit.

After we started the training, I understood why they asked certain deputies to be part of the training. There were quite a few applicants for the position. But they knew what they were doing when they picked certain people for the position. I think part of the reason they picked me was my comedy experience. I had been seen performing comedy at numerous department functions. They knew I had no trouble speaking in front of people. They knew of my experience facilitating for the DLI program. What they were most concerned with was finding applicants who could handle the amount of resistance that would be experienced trying to implement the training. Wow, was there a lot of resistance.

The consultants handled the training of executives, and we were trained to implement the training to the rank of sergeant and below. The consultant firm was getting $50,000 a month to work with the department in designing new testing for promotion. They had been working with the department for over 15 years on this. The department had already paid out 20 million dollars for this lawsuit by the time our group came in to implement the sexual harassment policy. People came into the training really pissed off. Right from the time, they came in the door. Some people had to be turned away and sent back to their unit to be rescheduled for another time. I was not prepared for the degree of pushback on this policy.

We had been trained very well on how to facilitate the training. In fact, we had to be approved by the consultants and report to the court that we had met the standard for facilitating the policy. We knew the policy inside and out. We knew how to facilitate it the way we had been trained. But we didn't have all the answers that we would get during the training. I didn't like that. I started studying sexual harassment and discrimination law on my own. I can honestly say that about a year into the training, I was a subject matter expert. I found out it was the law that for every sexual harassment policy to be defensible in a harassment case, the head of the company or business has to relay that they understand the policy, agree with it, and are dedicated to eliminating harassment based on sex, race, ancestry, gender, marital status, or medical condition. So to comply with this requirement, we showed a video of the Sheriff introducing the training.

Sergeants and deputies would get pissed off just seeing the Sheriff at the beginning of the training. It's a legal requirement that people take a test before the training and then after the training. And then each employee is to be given a written copy of the policy and sign for it. People would go off, "Why is the Sheriff making us sign for a copy? What, he doesn't trust us?" When I got a better understanding of the law, I was able to explain that this has nothing to do with the Sheriff; it's a legal requirement of a sexual harassment policy. Especially one where the business, in this case the department, had been found guilty of discrimination and policy implementation is part of a consent decree. This helped alleviate some of the anger in most cases, but not in all.

It was agreed to by the court that at the end of every training class an executive at the level of Commander or above would say a few words about the importance of the training, and that the department took it very seriously. And one day that executive was that same Commander who I talked to outside the Assistant Sheriff's office. I reminded him of our conversation. I told him, "You told me to go to DLI, and I did. I also became a facilitator for the training. You told me to go to a specialized operations unit, and here I am facilitating at the Equity Training Unit. Thanks for your advice. I know it will make me a better sergeant when I get promoted."

He said, "You did everything I told you to do, so when it's time, I will support your promotion." He had been my region commander, so I'm not sure how much input he had in promotions.

I do know that my personnel commander went out of her way to help me get promoted. She was my advocate. Everyone needs an advocate. I know because she actually called me from the promotion meeting. She said, "Cliff, I'm at the meeting now and we are on a break. I'm trying to keep you on the board and get you promoted. They want to take everyone off that doesn't have a degree. How close are you to getting your degree?" I told her that I was two classes short and I was taking those now. She said, "Ok, I'm going back in to fight for you." My personnel commander was Lynda Castro, and without her advocating for me I never would have been promoted. When she was my captain at West Hollywood, I took the time to stop at her office and chat whenever possible. Not asking for anything, just in passing. To make a connection. It really is about relationships. Lynda Castro, who I'm sure had to fight her way in rising through the ranks, always took the time to reach back and help others. I tried to follow that example after I was promoted. I never forgot what she did for me.

A few short months later an intent to promote list came out, and I was on it. I was promoted to sergeant in 2004. And almost all new sergeants who get promoted have to start their new assignments in the jail. Yuck, back to the jail. This is the worst. But it's only fair; there are sergeants who had to go back to the jail waiting for new sergeants to come in so they can go out to patrol. I was going to be in this group now. Back to Men's Central Jail I went, but now I was a sergeant. Just like when you go to patrol from the Jail, you first go to patrol school to prepare you for leaving the jail and going to patrol. Now my group had to go to Supervisors school and prepare us for our new assignments in the jail as a sergeant.

As much as Men't Central Jail was a nightmare to work as a deputy, it was as much or more of a nightmare to work as a sergeant. Although there were many negatives to working as a sergeant in the jail, there was just as many positives and, in fact, rewarding experiences. At the time when you are in the moment, it's hard to see the positives. At Lynwood Station, an executive once said to enjoy every moment. And he quoted Charles Dickens I think from his novel A Tale of Two Cities: "these are the worst of times, these are the best of times." When we're in it, it seems like the worst of times, and later we look back on such times fondly. I find that to be very true.

MENS CENTRAL JAIL

I ended up being the supervisor on the 5000/6000 floors. These floors had dormitories as opposed to cell blocks. In most cases, the inmates were in for lighter type crimes. Part of the 5000 floor housed what they called K11 classified inmates. They were gay and/or transgender. They were housed on one end of the 5000 floor and had to be kept away from the general population of the jail, which wasn't always that easy. Some of the transgender inmates looked anatomically like a woman, but they all had a penis. If they came into the jail taking female hormones, the county was required to keep giving them their hormones. Some of these inmates had very large breasts with long hair, and they made their own makeup. They took up two full dorms at one end of the 5000 floor. There were about 200 K11 inmates at any given time. Friday nights they would have a beauty show. The inmates would take blue medication pills and wet them to make blue eye shadow. They did all sorts of things with what they found in the jail to use as beauty products. Although it was prohibited by jail rules, let alone against the law, there was a lot of sex going on in those K11 dorms.

As you can imagine, I had to be very careful what deputies I assigned to work that part of the jail. For religious reasons alone, many deputies could not work around these inmates. There were two deputies assigned specifically to deal with the classification of the inmates who were assigned to these dorms. They would conduct interviews with each inmate prior to being assigned as a K11. Many inmates would try and lie their way in. They would claim to be gay so they could get assigned to these dorms for sex purposes. If an inmate was truly gay, they had better know the gay clubs and community to a certain extent, or they would not be assigned to the gay and transgender dorms.

There was a major political connection between the city of West Hollywood and the K11 section of the jail. Community leaders would donate televisions and whatever they were allowed to donate specifically for the K11 section. These leaders would tour the jail to make sure what they were donating was getting to the right inmates.

These inmates would go to a classroom in the jail and get

computer classes taught by an outside teacher that would come into the jail. Also, there were weekenders that would come into the jail on Fridays and serve their time until Sunday night. There were many outside clergies that would come into the jail to give services. This was the main way that drugs were brought into the jail. The weekenders would secrete the drugs in the cheeks of their ass to smuggle them in. They would swallow balloons of heroin, and once in the jail, retrieve them from their stool after going to the bathroom. They would put needles and drugs in plastic cigar holders, and then insert that into their ass to smuggle the needles and drugs into the jail. It was surprising the amount of drugs that would circulate inside the jail. No doubt many of the teachers, clergy, doctors, and psychologists that came into the jail would bring drugs in with them. Sometimes they would get caught, but most of the time they wouldn't. The head executives discouraged as much as possible any searches of people coming in and out of the jail. Everything they brought in as far as property would be thoroughly searched, but a pat-down of their person was hardly ever done.

I had a good crew on the 5000/6000 floors and liked all the deputies I had working for me. Our side of the jail was considered the soft part of the jail. In a lot of ways, we were looked down upon for working that side of the jail. I didn't like that. On every shift, we had an in-service form. This listed all the positions in the jail and who was assigned to them for that particular shift. Every shift had an extraction/emergency response team designation. It was usually six or seven deputies and a sergeant. When I was assigned as the sergeant for the emergency response team, I took that as an opportunity for the deputies in the rest of the jail to see what I was about.

One pm shift, the extraction team was called to the hardcore 3000 floor for an extraction, and I was the sergeant. There was a row of cells that housed a group of Southsider gang members. All these cell rows had what they call a shot caller on the row. All the inmates on that row took orders from the shot caller. When the team and I arrived with our helmets and shields, the lieutenant was negotiating with the shot caller. Sometimes it was just embarrassing the way the administration tried to negotiate with these gang members to avoid a major jail disturbance. It might come down to the lieutenant pleading with the shot caller, "Please don't cause trouble, we will get everybody ice cream." This was rare. Most of the time, you would have a lieutenant with some balls who wasn't afraid to make decisions and maintain control of the jail.

On this particular shift, the inmates on the row refused to submit to a cell search. My team, the floor sergeant and assisting deputies were in the hallway while the lieutenant was talking with the shot caller. I heard the shot caller tell the Lieutenant, "No, too many searches. No more. We are not going to allow any more searches of the row for a while." This back and forth went on for some time.

The lieutenant told the shot caller, "The team is waiting to come in, tell everyone to hook up (submit to handcuffing) and then no one gets hurt, and I will be here to supervise the search."

The last thing I heard the shot caller say, raising his voice so all the other inmates could hear, was, "Bring on the fucking team, let's get hurt. Nobody is hooking up, what are we waiting for."

Now on my team, I have a taser deputy, two pepper ball gun deputies (paint ball guns that shoot balls filled with pepper-spray), two shield deputies, a distraction grenade deputy, and two handcuff deputies. There is a video deputy designated to video tape the entire extraction process. Waiting in the hallway are medical personnel to administer aid to the inmates. We basically go in and start at the first cell, which in this case was the shot caller. I couldn't wait to take this guy out of his cell. Orders are given for each inmate to back up to the cell door so they can be handcuffed.

This wasn't going to happen since the shot caller had given the order that nobody is to hook up. So as we entered the row and went to the first cell, the other fifteen or twenty cells start yelling and throwing objects at the team. They had cups filled with urine and shit they threw at us. They threw toilet paper soaked in shit and urine. They took towels and jammed them down the toilet and start repeatedly flushing to flood the row with water. They want the floors flooded so deputies had a hard time getting their footing.

To suppress this barrage of fecal matter, deputies start firing pepper balls toward the end of the row. Inmates tie towels and sheets around their nose and mouths to try and minimize the effect of the pepper balls. We also have basically a pepper-spray cannon that shoots a powerful twenty to a thirty-foot stream of pepper-spray. As the inmates refused to be handcuffed, we deployed pepper-spray. If they were armed, we attempted to disarm them with the taser before we rushed in with takedown deputies. We pinned the inmates to the back of the cell, bringing them down and handcuffing them. Deputies removed them from the cell to the hallway for medical treatment if necessary, and then we moved on to the next cell.

This was my first extraction, so before we entered the row, I told them we don't get hurt—they do. They dictated how this is going to go, so be aggressive and take care of business. I was at the rear of the team, directing them as we went cell to cell. At one point, I jumped in to assist with the takedown of a giant inmate who wasn't going down. They really didn't need me, but I wanted them to know I was there to mix it up with them if need be. We had to tase about ten inmates that day. The south siders sent their message.

After the extraction of all the inmates from their cells, a search was made of the cells and all their property. Each inmate was interviewed on video tape by the floor sergeant and Lieutenant. I have to give these Southsiders credit; each one was interviewed and asked what happened and how they got their injuries. Each one would say on camera that nothing happened. We would even say on camera, "You refused to leave your cell, a deputy tased you, pepper-sprayed you and took you down to the ground. It looks like you have a black eye and a bruise on your forehead from the deputies."

And the inmate would say, "No, I fell. The deputies didn't do anything." I have to give them credit; they never made a complaint. Every once in a while, they had to make a statement and basically take an ass whooping to maintain street reputation.

Now, after all the fun and games were over, I had to create a force package. On a major extraction like this one, it might take a full week or two. I had to document from the beginning everything that was done up to my team entering the row and using force. I had to document each use of force by each deputy on each inmate at each cell in chronological order. I had to make sure each deputy prepared a

153

report on what they did and why. I made sure that all force was at my direction. Most of the time, I had to go over the videotape to remember who did what and when. I might have to remind the deputy that he used pepper-spray first, then a taser, and then a takedown, and then forced handcuffing. In the midst of the chaos, it's sometimes hard to remember exactly each move you make. As we take one inmate out, we are on to the next cell. And we do this for fifteen or twenty cells. Each one goes a little differently. Some inmates do submit to handcuffing, but most go with what the shot caller said, which was not to comply with any orders.

So, I had to gather all the reports from all deputies on the team. All the medical reports that dealt with each injury from the extraction. Submit all the reports with videotaped interviews to the watch commander. So this might take a week or two to get everything in order. In the meantime, it's not unusual for you to be involved in another extraction or several other force incidents. It wasn't unusual to be backed up five or six force reports. Then you might go a week or two with no force incidents, and you could get caught up. In the meantime, you had inmate complaints to handle and write up, and employee evaluations that were time-sensitive. And the Captain would want to know why the sergeants weren't walking around checking on the deputies. Quite a crazy place. There were sergeant positions in the jail that were considered premier that some didn't mind working for years and had no desire to go out to patrol. Most of us couldn't wait to get out of the jail and to a patrol assignment.

PATROL SERGEANT

When the time approaches where you can get out of the jail and transfer to patrol, you have to be proactive and interview at the stations you would like to work. Some stations would not take any sergeants unless they had interviewed at that station and been given the interview score of acceptable. Once the Captain gave you an "acceptable," they would have to take you as your time came up and they had an opening. Sometimes the Captain would bluntly tell you he or she couldn't rate you as acceptable because they would have to take you next, and they might be looking for someone else to bring to the station. Everybody was gaming the system to move personnel around to their liking.

My dream job would have been to go back to the Universal substation out of West Hollywood. In most cases, they didn't like to bring new sergeants to an assignment they worked at as a deputy. It creates difficulty sometimes when you have sergeants supervising deputies they worked with as peers before promoting. In most cases, they tried to avoid that. But it wasn't a hard and fast rule. Usually, sergeants that were at Universal stayed there, and the turnover wasn't very often, so I didn't think I had much chance to go back. So, I interviewed at other units.

I had taken sailing lessons in Marina Del Rey, and I had met a deputy who lived on a sailboat. He worked at the Marina Del Ray Station, which was right on the water. They had a separate Harbor Patrol that worked out of the station. I talked to the deputy who lived on the sailboat. I remember talking with him. "Let me get this straight. You live on this sailboat, and when you go to work, you get on your dingy and motor to the station dock and go to work?"

He said, "Yeah, it's a cool thing."

I interviewed with the Captain at the Marina who I knew from previous assignments. It would mean an hour commute from my house each way, but I didn't care about that. I stepped out the back door of the station, which was the dock that looked out over the Marina. I was in awe, taking in this wonderful sight when a lieutenant stepped out on to the dock with me. It was my training officer Marv Washington. He was now a lieutenant. My chance of getting to the Marina Station was getting better. So I felt good about my chance of getting to the Marina Station.

Shortly after I interviewed at the Marina, I got a call from Sergeant Talmo at Universal, and he asked me if I would want to come back to Universal. Are you kidding me? That would be a dream come true, but I didn't think it could happen. He said, "We've had a sudden opening, and I'll talk to Captain Long, and if Chief Ronnie Williams approves it, we will make it happen." Wow, I was getting excited about all this.

The list came out, and I was scheduled to go to the Marina Station. I got a call from Sergeant Talmo asking me if that was my choice. I told him that Universal was my first choice, and when I interviewed at the Marina, I told the Captain that my first choice was West Hollywood/Universal. Sergeant Talmo said that the Chief thought my first choice was the Marina. He called the Chief and had it straightened out. And I was on my way back to Universal, this time as a sergeant.

Universal was similar to the jail in that there were a lot of force reports for supervisors. Universal was a little more predictable. Weekdays were mostly quiet, and use of force incidents rare. Most of the force happened on the weekends late at night. So you could get caught up during the week, so when the weekend rolled around, you were ready for the nighttime fun. If force happened during the week, it would be later in the shift after 8 pm. The weekday shifts were usually ten-hour shifts, 4 pm to 2 am, or 5 pm to 3 am. A few days a week there would be two sergeants on. So, there was always an opportunity to catch up on the paperwork.

Things were going smoothly at Universal, and I was having as much fun as a sergeant as I did as a deputy. I got a call from a friend of mine who I had worked with at Universal who was now a Lieutenant. He asked me if I wanted to be a Lieutenant. I hadn't thought of it, but it was one of those calls that I thought I better say yes to. He said that an executive who had worked Region Two with us wanted to make sure that the former Lynwood deputies had equal opportunities to promote. He believed most of the deputies with a lot of field experience had little administrative knowledge, and this hurt their chances of promotion. So, he wanted to make sure those deputies had a chance to work an administrative position to be on equal footing with the deputies whose career was heavily weighted in administrative jobs.

When I told my friend that I was interested in promoting to Lieutenant, he said that I should be prepared for a transfer to an administrative spot, most likely recruitment or backgrounds. A few months later, shy of two years at Universal, I was transferred to personnel division as a sergeant in recruitment.

PERSONNEL DIVISION

I headed up a team of recruitment deputies at a time when recruitment was in high gear. The department had been given something in the neighborhood of 4 million dollars toward a nationwide recruitment campaign. We had a lieutenant, two sergeants, and about fifteen deputies. One sergeant was responsible for media and buying advertisement with part of our budget. I was responsible for recruitment from events and holding satellite tests. We had billboards all over the country. We had a big billboard as you drove into Las Vegas. We were on scrolling screens on busses in Chicago, New York, and Atlanta. We were on scrolling screens in baseball stadiums all over the country. We had ads on the sides of busses. The goal in the personnel division was to hire 1,000 deputies a year for three to four years. We were down about 2,000 deputies, and we lose about 500 deputies a year to attrition. Part of that plan involved recruitment advertising. Part of it was conducting tests all over the country. Testing involved the civilian division of personnel responsible for testing. They had to conduct the testing in compliance with civil service and California P.O.S.T. Peace Officer Standards of Training. We would send recruiters to colleges to give talks to upcoming graduates who would be entering the job force. We would follow up those talks with testing at the colleges. We had different strategies of recruitment depending on what community we were recruiting from. We sent a team of deputies and civilian testing employees to the gay and lesbian police Olympics in Chicago. We had gay deputies go and represent the department at these events. The department went to great lengths to make sure the demographics of the department reflected the demographics of Los Angeles County.

The other division in personnel involved in the major hiring process was the background division. They had a lieutenant, several sergeants, and about fifteen to twenty background investigators. The two divisions didn't work too closely, and it appeared to be by design. Someone called me and wanted to know what the current policy was regarding marijuana use. They wanted to know based on their recent use if they should bother to apply or not. I called a background sergeant and asked him. He told me he couldn't give me that information. He said it changes all the time, and they believe if they give out the current standard, applicants will lie to conform to the policy and avoid being disqualified or have to wait in going forward with their application. In retrospect, it makes sense. At the time it ticked me off.

We were recruiting at places that didn't make any sense to me. Recruitments goal was to test so many people within a certain time. The more we could test, the better. I would not have been surprised to see us testing people outside prison, as inmates were released just to get our numbers up. When I questioned the caliber of people we were testing, I was told that our job was to recruit and test, and it was Background's job to determine their qualifications. Common sense started getting in the way of my success at personnel. It wasn't as simple as looking for the best-qualified applicants.

After talking with two of the current academy classes, the Sheriff walked into recruitment spouting, "Where are my blacks! I want more blacks!" He was very upset about the lack of black representation in the academy classes. I was a little miffed about that. I don't know how much more we could do. I think eight or nine of my fifteen or so recruiters were black. We were heavily recruiting in the black community. We were constantly under pressure to test more and more people. Everyone was constantly aware of the numbers. I liked all the deputies on my recruitment team, and I think we were doing a great job. My decisions were constantly being undermined, which hampered my effectiveness as a leader.

Two of my black deputies called me after being assigned a recruitment event. It was advertised as a battle of the bands in Compton. The deputies called me and said, "Sarge, we researched this event coming up, and it is basically a group of gang members jamming. It's a waste of our time to go and set up a recruitment booth at this event." I told them I couldn't agree more and told them to cancel that event.

A lieutenant called me later and told me that he had advised my deputies that they were back on that event. He told me, "Cliff, if the Chief found out we canceled a black event, he would have my head.

159

Never cancel a black event no matter what it is."

Sometimes I would go home shaking my head. My team was getting stressed out. I did my best to send the message that if we didn't show up for work the next day, nobody would die. As opposed to working the field, where if we don't show up or do the right thing people die. I don't think the powers above me liked that I was sending that message in an attempt to get them to relax so they could perform better.

Some good things did happen while I was working recruitment. One night I was home, and I got a phone call just before midnight. The voice on the other end said he was the Sheriff's driver. He went on to say, "I don't know who you are, but Norm Crosby the comedian was scheduled to perform at the Sheriff's luncheon tomorrow, and he canceled. The Sheriff said to call you, and you would take his place." I told him that I would be there. He told me that I would be sitting on the dais with the Sheriff, his wife, and two other executives. I had a recruitment meeting scheduled that day in West Hollywood, so I wasn't supposed to be at the Sheriff's luncheon. I arrived at the Sheriff's Luncheon, which is an annual event. The Sheriff had just been reelected the previous week.

The ballroom was filled with over 800 members of the department. I loved seeing the looks on everyone's faces as they looked up at the raised dais from their tables. They see the Sheriff, his wife, a couple of executives, and Cliff Yates. I know they were thinking, What is he doing there?

I had been racking my brain most of the night trying to come up with a great opening line, but nothing came to mind at the time. It wasn't until I was introduced and stepped to the podium that a brilliant line came to me. I said, "We're in California and we have some terrible tragedies, fires, earthquakes, flooding, but last week we had a landslide that was fantastic; the reelection of Sheriff Baca!" And everyone in the ballroom jumped to their feet and gave the Sheriff a ten-minute standing ovation. The Under Sheriff leaned over and whispered to me, "That was great." I told a few jokes and then introduced the Sheriff. I have to say that was one of my great moments.

More and more, I did not fit in with this assignment. We sent a big contingency of deputies that would be assigned to the Pomona Fair. For years they had a recruitment video that would be on a loop at the booth. It was really inspiring. It showed all aspects of the Sheriff's Department and all the exciting jobs. It had shots of the beach team, deputies repelling out of helicopters, K9 officers in action. Deputies riding quads down the beach. Search and rescue teams repelling in the canyons rescuing stranded hikers. The harbor patrol and dive team, all to the soundtrack of "I Love L.A." by Randy Newman.

Another sergeant told me not to send that video, that there was a deputy in the video the Sheriff never wanted to see again. I had one of my deputies bring me the video. The deputy in question was on screen for about six seconds. I'm thinking because of those six seconds we are not going to show the video. I told my deputies that I was making the decision to show the video. I told them to take it to the fair. A mole found out about this and told on me. A lieutenant called me and said, "Cliff, I took the video; it can't be shown anywhere that the Sheriff might see it." As far as I know, the video was never seen again. Another decision overturned. I worked in patrol for over twenty years, and I don't even remember one of my decisions being overturned. Here I was in recruitment, and I was being undermined on a daily basis.

We were testing in the Santa Clarita Valley. We were short on deputies conducting interviews after the written test, so I filled in to help out. I was told you needed two deputies interviewing to disqualify someone, but one deputy interviews were conducted when we were short. And if there was a problem with the candidate, they would be invited back for a second interview with two interviewers.

I was conducting an interview by myself and asking the questions in the order they are supposed to be asked. When I asked the candidate, who appeared to be Middle Eastern, about working weekends, he said, "No, I can't under any circumstances work Sundays." I asked him about working with women, and he said, "No, I would never work with a woman." There was one more question that he gave a ridiculous answer to, something like he could never shoot anyone. I told the applicant that this was not the job for him and that he was disqualified.

I turned his folder over to the civilian employees who conducted the written test, and they said, "Sergeant Yates, you can't disqualify an applicant on your own. It takes two interviewers."

I was furious, and I said, "I'm a sergeant on the department. If I can't disqualify an applicant for these answers, what good am I?"

There's a line from Clint Eastwood in one of his Dirty Harry movies. "Personnel, personnel is for assholes." I couldn't agree more. Personnel was not for me. My success was all in my hands, and I alone am responsible for not succeeding. My direct lieutenant was in support of me all the way and tried his best to help me succeed. And he also arranged several interviews with other special units. But I sensed the powers who gave me the opportunity to use my personnel assignment as a stepping stone to promotion were not happy. So, I was promptly transferred back to Men's Central Jail. Most of the rumors were that I was kicked out of personnel. Which really wasn't the case. But I was happy to be out of there.

MEN'S CENTRAL JAIL 2

I was moved out of personnel at the same time as several other supervisors. It was looked upon by most that we all got rolled up and kicked out of personnel. I knew that wasn't the case for me; my lieutenant had arranged for me to interview at several specialized units. But now that I write this and relive the memory, maybe that was all smoke and mirrors, and I actually was booted out with the rest.

I was feeling a little down after being transferred. Had I gone to a patrol or a specialized unit assignment, it would have felt more like a lateral move. I always hated working in custody and saw this as a move backward. These are the times when personal development skills and the ability to change your state come into play. Some other sergeants and I were discussing the condition of the jail gym, which in its heyday would have been considered state of the art for a jail facility. It had a sauna that wasn't working. Two treadmills and one wasn't working. When I first came to the Sheriff's Department and was assigned to Men's Central Jail in 1984, I remember what a great looking gym it was. Almost 25 years later and nothing had been improved, and little maintenance seemed to have been done.

Somebody mentioned that there was a gym fund with over $7,000 in it. We checked with the civilian employee who was in charge of the gym and the fund. He confirmed the existence of the fund, and the money was still in the account. I gathered a few of my fellow sergeants and some deputies, and we formed a gym committee. I thought of this as kind of a mastermind group. We had a mission to renew the gym. I will say it was my initial idea that we could redo the gym and make it great again, but it was the rest of the group who came through with ideas and resources that made things start to happen.

We went through the gym and decided what we wanted and what we saw that needed to be fixed. We came up with a goal to raise enough money so that the gym committee had $12,000 to work with. I produced a comedy show to raise money. We had several jail barbecues to raise money, and in a few short months, we exceeded our $12,000 goal. We had one deputy who was a real wealth of knowledge, skill, and resources. He had worked in construction. He had access to a tractor-trailer, and he arranged to remove all the equipment and have it powder coated for minimal cost. While most of the equipment was out of the gym, we had a new floor installed. This was nice flooring, from what I remember it ate up about $6,000 of our budget. My go-to deputy used to install mirrors. We bought mirrors that he installed on the walls of the gym.

One of my fellow sergeants while working the Compton station made a friend who sold exercise equipment wholesale out of a big warehouse in south L.A. We went down there and picked out five or six treadmills and some weight equipment. The guy gave us all the treadmills and equipment for about $1500.00. The county agreed to come in and replace all the ceiling tiles. The sauna was repaired by replacing some part that I think cost about $100. It could have been replaced years before.

The gym looked so amazing when it was finished that we had a grand opening of the "New" gym. We had a big ceremony, and the Undersheriff came to cut the ribbon to the new gym. We really made a difference that people are still enjoying today. That was a highlight and a great moment of my second sergeant tour of Central Jail.

I was the supervisor on the 3000-floor one-midnight shift. It seemed like a night like any other night. The deputies were required to walk the rows and document their walks. One row on our floor had a dangerous and high-security row of cells. The front of these cells were covered in plexiglass and then a narrow row to walk in, and then a row of bars, with a walkway on the outside of the bars. The deputies were required to make a walk every half hour. There was a paper log of the checks, and also a paper on the wall at the end of the row with a bar code. The jail was going to a new system where the deputies would scan the bar code on their walks to record the time and location. At the time the walks were also still being documented in a logbook.

Although not required to do so, I, as a supervisor, made a walk down the row and recorded it in the log. Later that morning, an inmate was discovered hanging in his cell. Deputies cut him down from the sheet he was hanging from and called for medical personnel. They tried to revive him, but he was pronounced dead. When the crime scene was established and homicide detectives were called, deputies came forward and reported to another sergeant that they had lied about doing their security checks. They had a duplicate of the barcode at the end of the row and scanned the paper with the duplicate barcode without actually making the security check.

It was later discovered that the deputy assigned to the module where the inmate hung himself had signed out a patrol car to make a meal run. He came back and then went to the gym for about two hours. The inmate who died had attacked deputies and had been evaluated as needing a psychological evaluation. Because of a backup in the psych unit, he had been waiting to see a psychologist when he committed suicide. This suicide was prominent in the news that joined a long line of bad press regarding conditions in the jail. When the board of supervisors heard of the case, they put pressure on the department to make sure that a supervisor on the floor is severely punished as an example. That was me. The department imposed some severe discipline on me.

One thing was for sure; I needed to get out of Men's Central Jail. This was going to be tough as transfers were usually held up for personnel with pending discipline. Luckily I had made some good relationships with the right commander and the Captain of Transit Services Bureau (TSB).

I was able to secure a transfer and get out of jail. I was excited about my new assignment.

LAST ASSIGNMENT

Sometime in 2010, I transferred into the Transit Services Bureau. This turned out to be a great assignment. Not only was it a patrol assignment, but it also had a great amount of area with little restriction. The TSB had enforcement responsibilities for all the light rail and subway lines in the county. And also the bus lines and Metro Link trains. This gave us patrol duties throughout the City of Los Angeles, and numerous points, north, east, west, and south. We had the blue line which ran above ground from south L.A. To downtown where it went underground to Union Station. We had the redline subway which ran underground from Union Station to North Hollywood. We had the gold line which ran above ground from Union Station to Pasadena. We had the green line which ran above ground Norwalk to the west side, not quite to LAX. The Metrolink line went from Union Station north to Acton, east to San Bernardino, south to San Diego.

We had deputies who rode the trains, and deputies in cars that responded to calls for the buses. Deputies in cars could also respond to calls at the various subway stations. There was a south division and north division each with their own captain. It was quite an operation. Since I had originally applied to the New York City Police Department before leaving Livingston County, I knew this assignment would be the closest thing to working a NY subway system. My wife and I enjoy using the NY subways when we visit each year during the Christmas season, so I was anxious to learn about the Los Angeles system.

I mostly worked the overnight shift, which ran from 9 pm until 5 am. For the bulk of my time, I worked the north division and supervised deputies who patrolled the red, gold, and north end bus lines. In some weird agreement, we had patrol responsibilities for half of Union Station and LAPD the other half. For the most part, all calls for services in Union Station were handled by us.

* * *

For some reason, stepping in front of an oncoming train is a preferred choice of those wanting to commit suicide. It's always a brutal scene because of the moving train and devastation to the body. A lot of the time, the body is cut in half. In the short time I was at TSB, I know we probably had ten or more suicide by trains that I know of. Sometimes there were accidental deaths because of people walking on the tracks at night or their vehicle was stopped on the tracks.

I loved patrolling through downtown Los Angeles. They had some big redevelopment operations that beautified most areas of downtown. They created a big entertainment zone called L.A. live, which incorporated the Staples Center and the L.A. Convention Center. The area was full of restaurants and clubs. The downtown area was growing with the creation of trendy residential lofts. This was back in 2010-2013. The area east of Spring Street was the beginning of Skid Row. It was horrible, just stacked full of garbage and homeless in tents up and down the sidewalks. On the weekends church groups would come to the area in large numbers to hand out clothing, blankets, and food. I think this led to more and more southern Ca. homeless coming to Skid Row. There was the mission, which was always overcapacity, and people would wait for an opportunity to get in.

I remember driving my stepson through the area, and he was in shock when he saw how these people were living. The amount of garbage on the street was horrendous. But the city was keeping them in this corner just a few blocks away from the glitz and glamour of the revitalized L.A. I know it got worse as the years have gone by. But in 2019, when it became an epidemic of drugs and diseased rats, the national news started putting a spotlight on it. Seeing some of the news coverage, much of the area conditions were in effect back in 2010. Nobody wanted to hear anything about it. As soon as the national news started their coverage, putting shame on the city of L.A., all of a sudden everybody was clamoring to do something about it.

I was still doing some comedy during my time at TSB. I would perform on occasion at the Downtown Comedy Club which was operated by my good friend Kevin Garnier. I would say it was mostly a black club. Garret Morris was a regular at the club (1970's Saturday Night Live cast). I loved meeting and talking with Garret. He was getting up there in age, but was extremely energetic and still loved doing standup comedy. I produced a show in downtown and Garret agreed to host the show. He was amazing.

About two years before I retired in 2011, my parents came out to L.A., and I took them on a ride-along. We stopped in at the Comedy Club, and they were thrilled to have our pictures taken with Garret. A few short months later, Garret well into his 70's was cast in a supportive role in the now hit show Two Broke Girls. I was so happy to see him have such success late in life. I took my parents around to meet all of my deputies. We had a lot of great laughs that night—some of those deputies when I rarely see or talk to them ask about my parents. You wonder if your parents are really that wonderful and fun to be around. My parents really were loved by anyone that met them even for a brief time. Some of these deputies only talked to my parents for a few minutes, but they left a lasting impression.

June of 2010, the L.A. Lakers win another championship. I remember that night. I was doing a comedy show at Steven's Steakhouse south of the city and had permission to start my shift an hour late. I had just got offstage when my lieutenant called me and told me to get to work as soon as possible a riot was about to start after the Lakers' win. I never could understand the mindset of rioting when a team won. I could justify it in my mind if the team lost, but when they win? Can't understand the mentality of celebrating by burning down the city. We were heavily involved in the post-game activities because one of the major subway stops was a couple of blocks from the Staples Center.

I got in my uniform and immediately headed for the 7th and Metro Station where we had a command post. The large crowd was coming in our direction from the Staples Center. As the crowd got closer, more LAPD units and Helicopter Units arrived. The sky was full of police air units and all the local news station helicopters. Even though we were dead center in the heart of Los Angeles, the Transit Services Bureau was responsible for protecting the busses and their patrons, not the LAPD. It was a weird dynamic.

I was assigned a corner just east of Wilshire Blvd on 7th Street. Everything was looking pretty good on my corner until all of a sudden, it wasn't. People started gathering in large numbers on each corner. Cars were driving by with people hanging out the windows yelling and throwing things at the people on the corners. Two blocks away, the crowd started fires in the middle of the intersection. One block down they tipped over a taxi and started it on fire. I could see the flames from where I was standing. One of our Sheriff Units had made several arrests in connection with that fire.

All the crowds that had started from the Staples Center were now flooding the streets where I was posted. I had a team of deputies at the intersection, and we were ready to rock and roll. My team knew it was a green light from me to use whatever force was necessary to protect ourselves first, then whoever needed help. We never gave up or lost any ground at our intersection. But between intersections, there was no police presence.

Just down from where we were, the crowd stopped a bus in the middle of the street. They started pulling the bus driver from his bus through the side window. A response team ran by us firing paintball guns and distraction grenades, which quickly dispersed the crowd. They were running for their lives, and the bus driver was rescued before he could be pulled out of the bus.

This madness went on for a couple of hours. The crowd continued to burn cars and break windows out of businesses along the way. The crowd had left our area, and now LAPD was dealing with the rioters. We had stopped all bus lines and shut down all subway lines. A couple of hours later, we were able to reopen the subway stations and let the busses resume their routes. Kind of sad when you start hoping the local team doesn't win a championship, so you don't have to deal with the rioting.

I could see more and more that it was time for me to retire. As flexible and willing to change with the times as I was, I still had a hard time with the verbal abuse that deputies had to take. I couldn't get used to people verbally abusing deputies and the expectation that it was part of the job.

Transit Services is where I finished my thirty-year career with the Los Angeles County Sheriff's Department. It's a great feeling to make it to the finish line. I had told my friend at Livingston County in upstate New York before I left for L.A. "I would rather die of a gunshot than from boredom." I laugh when I think about that, but I have no regrets. It was my dream to work for a large metropolitan police agency, and my dream came true. I'm a little in awe that more than once since retiring I have run into deputies that worked for me, and they have said, "Working for you was the most fun I ever had on the Sheriff's Department." I've had a couple of co-workers tell me that same thing.

Out of all the wonderful things that I experienced in my career, I think hearing these words has the most meaning. To know you impacted and influenced someone in a positive manner is very rewarding. I have to say the thirty years went by in a flash. The department is so big, and if you move around to different assignments, you meet so many people. By the time you have moved around to several assignments, twenty years have gone by. I love the freedom of retirement, and I enjoy every day. Working for the L.A. Sheriff's Department was a very exciting and rewarding career. Things didn't always go as I wanted; there were several goals never attained. But many that I never dreamed of did come true.

I hope this book might find itself in the hands of someone who may have the thought of leaving their small little town and heading for the big city lights in pursuit of their dreams. For some who may have had a tough childhood or who aren't close to their parents and family, it might seem easy to make that decision. It wasn't for me. I was very close to my parents and love them with all my heart. I had a great childhood. I was an only child and was always encouraged by my parents. I had established myself with the Livingston County Sheriff's Department after five years of service. So, it was a tough decision to follow the yearning of something more is out there. But I don't regret it for a second. I found that the miles from home made me appreciate every visit and phone call. You can hop on a plane and be anywhere in the U.S. in four to five hours.

In pursuing your dreams, whether attained or not, you will become more, and you will be able to share more. Your relationships will be deeper and held tightly to your heart. Your family and friends will love coming to visit you. They will love sharing your adventures, and you will have many. You will have many adventures, loves, heartbreaks, but limited will be your regrets when you make the decision to follow your dreams.

FROM THE AUTHOR

I have been a cop by day and a comedian by night. I have produced a comedy special now streaming on Amazon. I have a talk show and a cooking show on Amazon. I am starting a podcast and continuing to write. The most rewarding moments have come by way of connecting with new friends. Join with me and share your adventure. Visit my web site and connect with me by joining my email group. Check out my videos and books at www.cliffyates.com

Made in the USA
San Bernardino, CA
30 November 2019